LITERACY LESSONS

DESIGNED FOR INDIVIDUALS

PART ONE

Why? When?
and How?

Learning to Read

I remember the look
of the unreadable page

the difficult jumble

and then the page
became transparent

and then the page
ceased to exist:

at last I was riding
this bicycle all by myself.

Cilla McQueen

LITERACY LESSONS

DESIGNED FOR INDIVIDUALS

PART ONE
Why? When?
and How?

MARIE M. CLAY

Heinemann

Published by Heinemann Education, a division of Reed Publishing (NZ) Ltd, 39 Rawene Road, Birkenhead, Auckland, New Zealand. Associated companies, branches and representatives throughout the world.

In the United States: Heinemann, a division of Reed Publishing (USA) Inc., 361 Hanover Street, Portsmouth, NH 03801-3912.

ISBN-13: 978-1-86970-322-6 (NZ)
ISBN-10: 1-86970-322-7 (NZ)
© 2005 Marie M. Clay
First published 2005
Reprinted 2005, 2006 (x3)

Library of Congress Cataloging-in-Publication Data
Clay, Marie M.
  Literacy lessons designed for individuals Part One: Why? When? And How?   / Marie
    M. Clay.
  p. cm.
Includes bibliographical references and index.
ISBN 0-325-00916-3
1. Language arts (Early childhood). I. Title.
LB1139.5.L35C545 2005
372.6--dc22
2005029876

Cover design by Brenda Cantell

Printed in China

The pronouns 'she' and 'he' have often been used in this text to refer to the teacher and child respectively. Despite a possible charge of sexist bias it makes for clearer, easier reading if such references are consistent.

The author and publishers permit the following record sheets in the Part Two Appendices to be copied by teachers for use with children. The commercial use of any of these record sheets is strictly prohibited.

Contents

Cautions

Most children (80 to 90 percent) do not require these detailed, meticulous and special Reading Recovery procedures or any modification of them. They will learn to read in classroom programmes of many different kinds. For a few children individual and consistent tutoring with these special procedures introduced after one year of instruction may well prevent the development of a pattern of reading failure.

It should be stressed that an early literacy intervention like Reading Recovery can be used with children from any kind of classroom curriculum. After a brief period of help, that is supplementary to the ongoing activities of the classroom, it brings the hardest-to-teach children to a level where they can be full participants in the curriculum adopted for that classroom. Because it is an individual intervention delivered only to the hardest-to-teach children, Reading Recovery cannot specify how a classroom programme for children of wide-ranging abilities should be mounted. One would not design a satisfactory classroom programme by studying only the needs of the hardest-to-teach children.

There are other groups of children who would probably also benefit from the use of Reading Recovery teaching procedures. It is because these procedures are designed for adapting the instruction to the learning needs of individual children that they can be applied to many beginning readers who are in some kind of special education. And, because the procedures allow for accelerated progress, they are particularly useful for young immigrant children entering English, or Spanish, or French programmes for five- to seven-year-old children.

Reading Recovery teachers need special training to make superbly sensitive decisions about how to interact with the responses of the hard-to-teach child. Children are hard to teach for many different reasons. This book provides a conceptualisation of how and why the teaching procedures are necessary, and it puts the main procedures into a text to be read. But how the teacher makes these procedures work for the individual learner with unusual patterns of responding is something that defies recording in a linear script of words. *A training course for teachers is essential.*

Each activity in the Reading Recovery lesson allows for a variety of competencies to be developed as the child engages in active problem-solving. There is no close match for Activity A to train Skill A. Each activity draws on literacy talents in a variety of ways. The outcome should be a child who has learned how to solve some of the mysteries of the coding system by his own efforts in either reading or writing.

From 1976 to 2005 Reading Recovery has developed infrastructure, different in different education systems, to ensure that the training of the teachers, and the delivery of instruction, and the outcomes within these different education systems have operated according to guidelines which ensure a high level of success. A large body of research has been accumulated, and new information becomes available each month. Every child's entry and exit and performance is documented in monitoring studies in each country.

A Reading Recovery training for teachers of special education children has been approved and supervised from time to time. If children require special individual instruction, help can be gained from Reading Recovery professionals in exploratory trials. The new title for this book acknowledges that these things have occurred and implies that further exploration of working with some special education children is appropriate. In each country there are trademarks which protect the quality of the delivery of a Reading Recovery Training Course and limit the use of the name to licensed deliverers of the programme. Trademarks are being applied for in each country for Literacy Lessons also. The holder of a national trademark should be consulted for advice, assistance and permission to undertake such exploratory developments. In the first instance developments should occur within the existing infrastructures for training provided in Australia, Canada, New Zealand, the United Kingdom, and the United States of America.

Changes may also be recommended, or approved, by the International Reading Recovery Trainers Organization (IRRTO). IRRTO is the organisation charged with maintaining the integrity of trademark Reading Recovery and guiding implementations across the world. Currently it elects a five-member executive board, giving equal representation to the five countries listed above, which support and monitor all participating trademark Reading Recovery interventions in all currently available languages (English, Danish, French, Spanish). The Executive Board of IRRTO has six major functions:

1) to carry out ongoing monitoring of implementations of Reading Recovery and require each national implementation to submit an annual report of their national data collection;

2) to respond to challenges to the implementation of Reading Recovery at the international level, and to specific national issues if these have international ramifications, according to IRRTO's international set of standards;

3) to support ongoing research in order to provide direction for change and growth in Reading Recovery through international collaboration and investigation;

4) to consider the ramifications for IRRTO member countries of a significant body of research findings;

5) to consider recommendations for changes in policy, implementation, and/ or practice of trademark Reading Recovery on the basis of international collaboration and research;

6) to oversee international developments including the introduction of Reading Recovery in a new country and/or redevelopment of Reading Recovery in another language.

1 A simple view of a complex theory

When a child first looks at a written code and tries to make something of it, this is a new experience for his brain which can already deal with oral language. The new task is about learning to recognise the visible symbols and making some invisible links to how we speak. How do we bring these things together?

Often people choose to explain the visible/invisible relationships by helping the child to link the smallest features of the letters with the phonemic features of the oral language. In my observations of young children trying to make any sense of the code I chose to define reading as a message-getting, problem-solving activity, and writing as a message-sending, problem-solving activity. Both activities involve linking invisible patterns of oral language with visible symbols.

When you think about it, deaf people learn to 'speak' with their hands, and blind people learn to 'read' with their hands. So the human brain is really quite flexible about how it can deal with linguistically coded messages on paper.

We are probably most aware of this linking process when we have a smattering of knowledge about a foreign language. We can use our visual sense, and we can learn some phonological links, but we only know what some of the words and phrases mean. We find ourselves searching hard for possible meanings.

Early literacy learning is something like that. As children get better at finding the links they look for more opportunities to engage in these activities. To make progress you must learn some rules about scanning the printer's code. Only then can you direct your language and visual perception to the problem of extracting a message from text.

How should we think about these scanning rules and the links we make? We can assume that we create networks in the brain linking things we see (print on a page) and things we hear (the language we speak). Messages flow in and out of those networks. In the context of reading and writing this is often called *literacy processing*. Familiar marks on the page can be linked to familiar language networks in the brain, and they allow us to make sense of novel messages never read before. Processing activities may involve only one network or many networks 'talking' to each other!

Educated people ask themselves questions as they read and write. We become aware of our questions when our answers fail to match with something on the page before us. Asking questions is a means of eliminating alternatives, in order to make a decision about what the print says.

After only a brief time at school children have acquired many ways of checking words in the text they are reading. They move from print to message and back at each decision point. Letter by letter, word after word, they select a response and begin to construct the phrase or sentence. From the word groups, they get meaning to aid the next bit of solving, and that helps them to solve the meaning further along the text. Probabilities or rules of occurrence are derived from our everyday experiences with texts. As the child reads, his brain links the sounds of speech and the squiggles on a page of print and computes the probability of information. Children construct their personal rules about written language from the print you expose them to.

The recommendations in this book follow from some assumptions. I assume that we are aiming to develop and explain effective reading and writing and therefore we need to observe what it is that successful readers and writers do (relative to their age and time in school).

I also assume that these processes are complex and will not be easy to observe and explain. We therefore need to be tentative and flexible because we could be wrong in our explanations from time to time, or from this pupil to that pupil.

The two activities of reading and writing are similar in many ways. It is useful to assume that working effectively in one activity will help with working in the other. I assume that they affect each other reciprocally, and that oral language is a further rich resource serving both those activities.

Most written language occurs as continuous text, so the focal task for the learner is to problem-solve the message(s) of continuous text. That is another one of my assumptions. Teaching a child 100 words, or 26 letters, in isolation, before you allow him to read a text does not seem like the appropriate learning context for laying down the foundational neural networks.

An explanation of literacy learning is, I believe, deeply embedded in psychological theories about what the brain can and does attend to, and about how easily something that has happened in the past can be recalled. Even more fascinating is how, when you are learning a complex thing a bit at a time, the pace at which you put it all together appears to be important. Negative effects tend to occur if you do a lot of reading and writing on the basis of a half-formed theory for too long. There are some interesting deep-level questions about these things that have yet to be explored.

An essay on 'Diversity and Literacy' by Emilia Ferreiro (2003) summarises what we have learned from research about the complexity of literacy learning. She concludes (pp. 72–73) that literacy is best acquired

a)   when students are allowed to interpret and produce a diversity of texts (for this acknowledges the diverse purposes for which texts are created);

b)   when students are provided with diverse sorts of interactive experiences with written language;

c)   when students are challenged by a diversity of communicative purposes and functional situations linked to writing;

d)   when the diversity of problems to be faced in producing a written message is acknowledged (problems with graphic representation, with spatial organisation, with the spelling of words, with punctuation, with lexical selection and organisation, and with textual organisation);

e)   when students are asked to work with texts from a diversity of viewpoints (author, proofreader, commentator, evaluator, actor); and

f)   when … it is presumed that the diversity of students' experiences enriches their interpretation of a text and helps them to distinguish between the exact wording and the intended meanings … (for) not all of them think the same thing at the same time.

Ferreiro has observed the literacy learning of young children closely — in Spanish, French, Italian and English — and I am sure she is not writing only about older children. She also has in mind the tasks we design for our young children.

Young constructive readers and writers work at problem-solving sentences and messages, choose between alternatives, read and write sentences, work on word after word, with the flexibility to change responses rapidly at any point. As they attend to several different kinds of knowledge, they are searching, selecting, rejecting, self-monitoring, and self-correcting.

Children use their brains to attend to certain things, to work out certain things, to find similarities and differences, to build complex processing systems, to use the language they already speak, and to link it to visual squiggles on paper. What has to go on in their heads is similar for children learning different languages although the item knowledge about the symbols, sounds and words, and the rules for structuring the languages will differ.

Challenged by texts children discover new ways to go beyond their current operating power and lift their literacy processing across a lifetime. Diverse activities are critical for extending processing power. Ferreiro's description of the complexity of reading and writing and the diversity of the texts they work with seems to me to apply to all three language versions of Reading Recovery.

Surprisingly, when we take our minority group (the lowest 20 percent of children near the beginning of their formal schooling) and provide short-term individual intensive care we can get an accelerated turnaround in learning which enables those children to catch up to their peers.

However, I know that the literacy processing systems constructed by learners during beginning literacy are massively influenced by the expectations and opportunities of the school curriculum and by the teaching practices of their schools.

2 The prevention of reading and writing difficulties

*L*iteracy Lessons *(Parts One and Two)* is a companion volume to *An Observation Survey of Early Literacy Achievement* (Clay, 2005). The Observation Survey introduces teachers to ways of observing progress in the early years of learning about literacy, and makes possible the early selection of children who may encounter difficulties. Teachers find that observing children, closely, helps them to fine-tune their teaching for beginning readers and writers who are very different, one from another.

I assume that literacy difficulties arise for many different reasons; some of these have to do with the experiences of the children so far (O'Leary, 1997); others have to do with the education delivered to a particular child with particular needs by a particular school system. *A preventive intervention in literacy learning must consequently address the extremes of variability that could affect any child learning to read or write.* Once formal instruction begins, what may be difficult for one child is not an indicator of what may challenge another child.

In the last century it became clear that the human brain had evolved for hundreds of thousands of years before man began to write language down, and that cerebral mechanisms evolved for vision and for spoken language long before it was necessary for man to deal with written language codes. Here are some extracts from a strong statement about this written by editors Breznitz and Share in a 2002 review of research on phonology.

> Reading acquisition in an alphabetic orthography is an activity lacking any evolutionary basis.

> An alphabetic orthography (is) only a recent cultural invention.

> The fact that the brain is not 'wired' for reading partly explains why reading does not come 'naturally' like speech or visual perception which both appear very early and universally in children's development.

In recent years research and debates have highlighted the importance, in learning to read, of the smallest units that change meanings in speech (the phonemes). Too little attention has been paid to how the young child's fast, effective systems for visually scanning the world become hooked up to these phonemes. Every language has its own set of phonemes: the number of sounds used by one language differs from that in another language, and the pronunciation of sounds differs in different dialects of any language. These differences in phonology make it difficult for me to pronounce some sounds in French, for example, or to understand the instructions of a Glasgow bus driver.

This guidebook is for teachers who are learning to deliver instruction to young children, individually, and supplementary to ongoing classroom instruction. The activities it recommends are designed for children who are clearly not making satisfactory progress during the first year or so of school. In particular it is planned for use in the training of professionals who already have a good record for helping such children make up for lost time. Within 12 to 20 weeks the children begin to contribute to their own learning and, once they have caught up to their classmates, they are expected to continue to progress effectively with their age group in subsequent years.

This text does not prescribe the teaching emphases or sequences step by step. Teachers must learn how to compile a series of lessons from the suggestions in this book to suit the individual strengths and weaknesses of each child, taking into account where that child is on a gradient of learning from simple to complex. How long the child's series of lessons needs to be depends on how quickly and efficiently the teacher can lift and expand the child's range of performances.

For children who differ markedly in their competencies and ways of responding, an individual teaching situation is the most efficient way to achieve the necessary changes. I am convinced that it is inefficient to teach more than one of these children at a time. The costs for up to 20 weeks of 30 minutes a day of individual tuition are not high if effective results can be achieved in very different education systems with the lowest-achieving young children. When an education system delivers individual instruction for 30 minutes a day, five days a week for 20 weeks, that teaching is equal to two full weeks of individual attention during school hours — a low price to pay as an insurance against literacy problems!

For the past century education systems have trained speech therapists to give individual instruction to preschool children who are not speaking well compared with others in their age group. This book introduces procedures to be used to recover a normal trajectory of progress in literacy learning in ways that are similar to the clinical help that is offered for oral language development for a few special children. It begins as soon as we can reliably identify that the child is falling behind his age mates.

Three steps to prevention

The first essential step towards reading and writing success is to have good preschool experiences available to all children.

Preschool children need to have interesting and challenging opportunities to develop their brains. Teaching 'literacy things' directly to preschoolers is not the solution to this challenge. You may think you need to prepare them for things you would like to teach them after they get to school but those things probably do not have the immediacy of other powerful preschool learning situations. Preschoolers need to explore their environments and share activities with interested adults. Highly motivating exchanges with the preschool world will be a sound preparation for taking aboard new kinds of experiences at school.

We can talk with preschoolers often about many different things, let them try to write when someone else is writing, read many kinds of stories to them, and respond when they try to 'read' books for themselves. We should also bring back those chants, songs, rhymes, raps and poetry that engage their interest. When they enter school those children will talk enthusiastically with others about their experiences. They will be cognitively aware, mentally alert, and looking for new things to do. All those things provide a good foundation for literacy learning.

Children who have grown up in a literate environment and have knowledge about books and print may seem easier to teach, but children who did not get such opportunities will learn these things very quickly if their brains are adept at taking on new experiences. Interesting and challenging opportunities to explore the world are an insurance against having difficulties once you get to school.

Some children will transition into school from homes or preschools that emphasise speaking and oral language. While that is a great preparation for literacy learning, it may be that an emphasis on oral traditions in some cultures has severely reduced exposure to printed language. If this is the case the school needs to deliver extra opportunities for engaging with print, approaching this with due cultural sensitivity. Other children entering school may have had great experiences with books in another language that is not the language of the school. Bridges need to be built for both these groups of new entrants to engage with books in another language. Too few schools build those bridges; too few schools plan for make-up opportunities.

Children who come to school speaking any language will have a preparation for literacy learning that is to be valued, whatever that prior language is. Research is clear that most children can add a second language at this age with relative ease, and, although it does not happen overnight, it does not take them long. We need to see them as competent children who speak and problem-solve well in their first culture and who are lucky to be learning a second language while they are young and active language learners. It is surprising how rapid their progress can be.

This is just as true when two different dialects of one language are being used. What teachers sometimes forget is that the school language environment impacts the child's learning for only a few of his waking hours, and the child's home and community language will still provide the majority of his language learning opportunities in the first years of school.

The second essential step in the prevention of literacy problems is to have a good curriculum for literacy learning in the early years of school taught by well-trained teachers. Most children will learn to read and write in the first years of school (in infant schools or junior classes or first grade classrooms).

However, encouraging active engagement with learning opportunities of all kinds in the preschool years, and providing good quality first teaching, are not enough. A third essential step towards reducing the numbers of children who might have lasting problems with reading, writing and spelling is to provide access to an early intervention for the lowest-achieving 20–25 percent of the age cohort. A small number of children who were not able to keep up with the terrific rate of progress of their peers can be helped by a different approach. Give them a short series of lessons that are individually designed and individually delivered by well-trained teachers. It will only take a short series of lessons before we see their progress accelerate and they learn to participate within the average group of children in their class without further individual support.

The third essential step involves three things:

- a check on every child's progress around the end of the first year of school,

- access to a second-chance intervention for the lowest 20–25 percent of the age group (together with increased attention among classroom teachers to the progress of the next 20 percent),

- and longer-term help for the few children whose problems were not all solved during the early intervention and for whom further individual help is deemed necessary. This should be no more than about 1–2 percent of the age cohort.

Further reading:
See Clay, *Change Over Time in Children's Literacy Development* (2001) and *An Observation Survey of Early Literacy Achievement* (2005) for further discussion.

On entry to school

At the beginning of schooling when children enter formal instruction the foundations are being laid for all their future interactions with education. Children need to emerge from these years with a control of the language of instruction. It is all profit and no loss to already speak another language that is not the language used in school, but those children will need *additional make-up opportunities* to use the new language of the school. They need to become the kind of readers whose reading improves because they read, and the kind of writers whose writing improves every time they write. Literacy learning provides the tools the child will need to underpin his future progress in education, and they are critical for success in the new information age.

What happens to the five-year-old children who come into the first classes of your schools? How are they grouped? When are they moved to another group? or to a new class? We know that children learn at different rates. What happens in those early days of school? How do we shift children from one level of competence to another? These questions are related to the quality of instruction given to the school entrants. There are great variations between schools in how they manage this path of progress. It is interesting to compare schools and education systems, noting differences in organisation and differences in the criteria used for moving children. We find different solutions in schools of different size, and variations from only one intake of new students a year to continuous entry after the fifth birthday.

Countries decide the age at which children start school on some arbitrary basis; for historical reasons, custom, or convention. Once a large group of children intermingle in their classrooms their lives will be different from what they would have been had they not come into formal education at that time. Simply by bringing them into formal education (whether they enter a reception class, or a developmental programme, or a strictly sequenced skill-teaching curriculum) we change the life opportunities for those children. Whatever the child has been able to learn before he comes to school, his prior learning goes through some transitions strongly influenced by the particular opportunities he is now exposed to by that school.

Teachers in first-year classes are charged with a common task — to bring children with vastly varied experiences in their preschool years towards some group performances in the classroom. Those teachers encourage new students to make a transition from old ways of responding to new ways of responding that can be used on academic tasks. The teacher has to draw into her instructional group the child who has limited control over language, and the one who is shy or withdrawn, and the one who is reluctant to try new things.

We invite children into formal education compulsorily by law. Teachers and schools are in control: they engineer the opportunities and create suitable transitions into school. The teacher of new entrants is not just minding the children until they mature, at which point they can be moved on to a teacher who is really going to do some work with them. That is far from the true situation. *These transitions from enormous variation in preschool experiences to standardised school procedures and a curriculum imposed by society may be more important than any later transitions that occur in children's schooling.*

The first school class is most important. Where do these first teachers learn their trade? How much help do they have when they first begin to teach children who are entering school? The more formal the school's instruction (engineered by the teacher to meet the education system's requirements), the more bewildered some new pupils can become. The teacher and the system must take into account that the child's prior learning may not have prepared him for many new experiences such as:

- how to work with a large group of children
- how to obey institutional rules
- how to meet the minute-by-minute demands of the teacher
- how to compete for her attention with other children.

How should the newcomer interact with this new complex environment and learn from it? The teacher of a new entrant class needs to know a lot about early childhood and the characteristics of young learners and the vast variations that can all lead to successful school progress. For children this first year at school is a very important time and the teacher who helps them make the initial transitions is a very important person.

In 1963–64 I watched 100 children's progress through the first year of school. I took records at weekly intervals of what they were doing and what they were saying. To give two examples of the long-term outcomes of their progress, one of the boys who went along fairly slowly for the first six months ended up with marks over 90 percent for six subjects in a national examination taken in the third year of high school. Another boy at the same school got into a terrible tangle in the first year, had severe reading problems, went to a reading clinic for several years but finally passed the same examination. That was a success story for the child but learning had been a trouble to him throughout his schooling, probably because of some inappropriate learning that went unnoticed in his first year at school. If only I had known then how to help him in his second year of school!

At the end of this research study I was saying that classes in the first year of school should ideally have a maximum roll of 20, and not more than 25. Smaller class numbers allow the teacher to meet each child where he is, arrange instruction so that he can proceed from his strengths and ensure that all children move into schooling without confusions and with a sense of success.

In New Zealand we have children entering school throughout the year as they reach their fifth birthdays. We recognise that all children will need to be read to, and will want to participate in talking about books, storytelling and dramatised stories. They will attempt to write down messages and stories during the school day. These children will start at different places, progress at different rates, and begin with a lot of exploring of print in their writing and in their attempts to reread simple storybooks. Some will do this almost on entry to school, others within a month or two of entering school, others not for half a school year, and some children needing close observation may not be doing this by the end of their first year of school.

There is considerable variation in the rate at which these New Zealand children move into simple little reading books. In my opinion, the explanation for these delays is not that the child is taking a year to mature but that he is taking a year to learn many things that contribute to laying the foundation of later success in schooling. Some children learned some of these 'things' before they came to school, some take about six months to learn them, some take at least a year. We now know that we can pick out the children at about six years of age who do not have effective control of beginning reading and writing behaviours that other children have learned.

If a teacher becomes a highly sensitive observer of slow-to-learn pupils, she can design instruction in ways that engage the children who are already confused. In Part Two of this book there are recommendations designed to help teachers make some necessary adjustments.

Educators have recognised in part some of the problems arising from these individual differences. They have altered the rate at which they introduce children to literacy learning but here I would inject a critical note. *I do not believe we have paid sufficient attention to designing the tasks and the instruction that we provide during that period. We offer standard tasks which do not meet the diversity of the students.* It is not only that these children are moving at different rates; some of them need more help with some aspects of the tasks than others. Surely that makes sense. We need to think more about children taking different paths to reach similar outcomes.

Unfortunately when teachers say of a child, 'He cannot make any progress in reading and writing' or 'He is not ready for reading and writing', too often that is only true if the school demands that he uses a particular curriculum approach. There is probably another route by which he could learn and in that case the instruction would start, not where the teacher is in her thinking, but where the child is in his learning.

Observing progress

To be able to detect how different the path has to be for individual children we will have to observe more closely than we have in the past what the five- to six-year-old is doing and what he is capable of. Some of my work has been directed towards providing teachers with some structured situations in which they can observe children's behaviour carefully, record with greater accuracy what they can do, and plan with insight instruction for what the children cannot do (Clay, 2005).

If there is no magical moment at which a child is 'ready' to learn to read or write what can we look for in the first year that indicates progress? I look for movement or change in the child's literacy behaviours. My criterion for progress during the first year of school would be that a child move from those responses he could give when he came to school towards some other goals that I see as appropriate for him. I am looking for movement in an appropriate direction from what he could already do at entry. Only careful monitoring will assure me that the child is not becoming confused and practising inappropriate behaviours. I have to watch what he is doing, and capture what is happening in records of some kind. Otherwise Johnny, who never gets under my feet and who never engages in activities where I can see what he is doing, may practise behaviours, day after day for a year, that will handicap his subsequent progress.

One critical area of early literacy learning is directional behaviour. The boy mentioned earlier (p. 9) who had some difficulty in passing the School Certificate examination was a boy who was quite confused about direction (or the serial order rules of written English) during his first year at school. At the end of the first year he was equally satisfied with moving from right to left across print as he was moving from left to right. Visual learning about what to expect to see in print must be seriously disturbed if you do not happen to scan English from left to right. By the end of the first year at school this boy had not established a consistent left-to-right visual survey of print. Organising to prevent reading failure depends a great deal on providing opportunities for observing what children are doing.

I would like to expand on this idea of observing. My emphasis on observing came from my work as a researcher rather than from my work as a teacher. The explanations in books did not seem to account for my successes with remedial work; what the children learned did not seem to emerge from what the theories suggested that I should teach. If I were to adopt a neutral stance and observe exactly what children did, I would have to step out of a teaching role and become much more like a scientist setting up a situation and recording precisely what happened. When I write of observing children closely this is what I mean. *There must be times when the teacher stops teaching and becomes an observer, a time when she must drop all her presuppositions about a child, and when she listens very carefully and records very precisely what that particular child can in fact do.*

To prevent reading failure teachers must take time to observe what children are able to do. This requires time out from teaching, time set aside for observing. The younger the child and the poorer the reader, the more time the teacher requires for recording what she observes and for thinking about what she observes. One must organise for such observation time. In this situation it is difficult not to prompt, not to help, and not to teach, but such activities do not have any place in the observation situation.

Observation involves more than hearing children read every day. It involves being a teacher who interacts with the child, who notices the child's responses to the story, its language and its meanings, and who takes the time to gather evidence of how the child is working on print. The teacher must be reflective and responsive to the negotiations of the child.

A check after one year at school

Knowing the pressures on teachers one has to be realistic. What would be the most economical time from the teacher's point of view to carry out thorough observation checks? What would be a good time to identify the children who are either confused or not making progress? I assume that the class teacher would observe her children as often as possible, from week to week perhaps. But drastic changes occur in children's lives. Children change schools or classes, they lose parents who leave the home, they have intermittent absences for health reasons. It is not sufficient to leave the decision to observe or not, to the class teacher. By the end of the first year at school somebody should be responsible for checking on progress towards effective early reading and writing.

I recommend this check be done at the end of the child's first year of formal instruction in New Zealand and around about six years of age in most of the education systems teaching in English. The child should be given sufficient time to adjust to the school situation and a variety of opportunities to pay attention to literacy activities. A classroom teacher who noticed that a certain focus in her curriculum did not suit a particular child would try another approach during the first year of school. A check around the sixth birthday maximises the opportunities, minimises the pressure on the child, and does not leave the child for too long creating habits of responding that might handicap him and be hard to unlearn. If we want children to catch up with their classmates who are racing ahead of them we cannot wait too long because it becomes increasingly difficult to bring children to effective classroom performance with their age group. The longer we leave children without supplementary help after the first year of school, the longer they will have to spend on supplementary instruction higher up the school.

A check on progress after about a year at school is to be recommended but it would need to be sooner if schooling begins at seven years because the older children seem to learn at a faster rate. We must organise to observe the ways in which change in literacy learning is occurring after one year at school for five- and six-year-old beginners, and after about six months into school for seven-year-old beginners. This early check has to be organised as part of the school's assessment planning, taking other factors like promotion or retention policies into account. If we can reliably identify some children who are falling behind their classmates and not yet engaging well with literacy activities, then we will need some very skilful teachers to teach those children.

The observation procedures identify the children who need help and they show where the areas of strength and weakness lie. It is important that the early intervention teacher has had experience with children who make normal progress before she begins to design different paths to similar outcomes for some children. She will design different fast tracks for children, taking their available strengths into account. In every school this calls for organising so that you can have staff with special expertise available for the children who find it hard to make the transition into literacy learning.

Teachers who work in an early literacy intervention should be given recognition for the work they do. The task is not quite as exciting as teaching children of varied talents in a classroom. It is a job that carries more strain, and one's pupils will often have lower achievement than those of other teachers at the end of the year. The school has to recognise that this person is very important and needs appropriate rewards for tackling this task. The response of these children may not be rapid, even when they are given a highly skilled and experienced teacher who uses special techniques.

Not all of them will make a spurt and catch up. Some children who have not really taken much notice of instruction in the first year may begin to take notice and learn quickly with individual tuition. Other children who have made little progress after a year at school are children who have unusual difficulty in learning spontaneously what most children learn but who can become literate with extra teaching directed to their idiosyncratic needs. A few children are trying to learn complex tasks with multiple counts against them.

What can one look for in early literacy in order to prevent failure? Let me make an analogy with mathematics and the changes we have seen there in recent years. Almost nobody considering the young child learning beginning mathematics is going to think in terms of how many arithmetical items he knows. Almost everybody will be thinking: 'What mathematical operations can he carry out?' Although we may not yet have definitive descriptions of all the strategic activities or operations that are acquired in early literacy this kind of shift in our thinking is happening.

In order to prevent early struggles with literacy learning we should be trying to understand how the child is using the information on the printed page and relating it to information 'in his head'. We have to observe him reading books: it is not enough just to check on his recognition of words in isolation. We can listen to a child correcting himself. He reads, he stops, and he goes back. Nobody suggested that he should do this. This activity tells us that he is in some way monitoring his own reading. If he is listening to what he is saying he may recognise that something does not fit, and, taking responsibility for solving the problem, he goes back to work on it again.

High-progress readers move into reading, respond well to classroom instruction and by the time they have been at school for about a year, they are monitoring their own reading in helpful ways. On texts that interest and challenge them they can teach themselves new things about working on that new material.

The child who is not able to do this monitoring of his own reading is the one who needs the teacher most. Teachers' observation records show that they allow good readers to read much more than they do slow readers. There are obvious reasons for this. The slow child takes longer to read, and he is reading much more limited text. The high-progress reader is reading involved text and reads many pages to get through an important part of the story. This suggests that if we simply organise to give the slow children twice as much time and attention as the good readers we might in fact be doing quite a lot to prevent literacy difficulties.

So it is important to bring children to the point where they can tutor themselves to some extent by monitoring their own reading. Situations must be set up where they can carry on without much attention from the teacher. This leaves her more time to work with readers making slower progress.

Advantages of individual instruction

A major problem that follows from this thinking about improving the transition into literacy learning for all children is the advocacy for individual instruction. Individual versus group instruction presents administrators with a dilemma. Formal education procedures are, of necessity, group procedures, but the best progress for a particular child will result from the kind of individual instruction that works with the child's strengths to overcome his weaknesses. A compromise between whole class teaching and individual instruction has been to teach children in groups of similar ability. This does not do away with the remaining challenge to meet unusual individual learning needs. If the learning is considered optional that would work. However, we cannot justify teaching all children as if all need the same kind of teaching, not *when the learning is an essential foundation to subsequent success in education. We will always need to make special provisions for some children.*

Teachers recognise great differences between children in their background experiences and personality traits. Historically we thought we could solve this problem by letting children come to literacy in their own time; some were allowed to take longer before starting their literacy learning and others were allowed to take longer to travel through the required early learning schedules.

We need to provide literacy instruction in ways that adapt more to individual differences. Much still remains to be done to change our teaching practices. Sometimes we need to provide individual one-to-one teaching in addition to the classroom programme.

There was a strong emphasis on individual tuition in the education system in Sweden in the early 1970s. One of the main regulations of the Swedish Education Act of 1962 and 1969 was that the personal resources of the individual child would be the starting point for the planning of education and teaching. According to objectives stated in the school law the school must stimulate the child's personal growth towards his development as a free, self-active, self-confident, harmonious human being. The school must give individual education.

Some steps taken in Sweden to further a diagnostic approach and that kind of individualisation of the teaching of reading were these:

- Class size was reduced to a maximum of 25 in the first three years — but the average size for the country as a whole for the first three years was between 17 and 18 children per class.

- Better opportunities than before were provided for individual tutoring, small group teaching, teaching in clinics and special classes of various kinds. In the first three grades, there was written into the teaching load of each teacher a weekly two-hour block of time for tutoring individual children from her class who, in her judgement, needed such help. Obviously there had to be organisation for this when it was part of the teacher's weekly work.

- Another procedure was to have one-half of the reception class or first-year class meet with the teacher for the first two hours of the day, with the second half arriving two hours later and staying on two hours later. This is an interesting way to reduce numbers and allow more individual instruction for children having particular difficulties.

These excellent rationales and practices were replaced in the 1980s in Sweden by new philosophies and different practices. In education we live with waves and cycles and fashions, returning to old ideas and forgetting what we have learned.

Observing children's early interactions with print and providing individual teaching for some children were recommended in Sweden in the 1970s. They remain imperatives.

Part Two of this book is focused upon individual tuition. Those who deliver successful early interventions to children having the most difficulty with literacy learning are watching with interest the mounting evidence arising from research on effective classroom teachers who work with small groups of children but respond to the needs of individuals in their small groups. They support, demonstrate, and rehearse very specific things that would otherwise prevent a child from taking aboard the focal point of the lesson. There is an increasing awareness among successful classroom teachers that some children can take different paths and yet reach the same standard, state-required outcomes.

In summary

Who are the children clearly getting left behind by the end of their first year at school? At the Ohio Reading Recovery Conference in the year 2000, P. David Pearson described them as the 'intractable', the 'hard to distinguish', the 'not responding well', and the 'would do well if they got the resources' children. To get these children off to a good start with literacy learning we have to provide:

- opportunities for new staff to learn to observe children and discuss their progress with colleagues who are specialists in early literacy learning,
- opportunities for teachers to learn to observe how a child is working on texts and how to support his processing of the information in print,
- an education system in which teachers and schools find out which children need supplementary help to build a sound foundation for literacy learning before the end of the first year at school, and
- resources for teaching 20–25 percent of young children individually for a short period of time.

There will always be a challenge to meet individual differences when children enter school because at that time children are very different in so many ways. Teachers must be observant of individuals' responses and of individual progress. They must be aware that alternate and different learning sequences can lead to progress, but it is most important to know when progress is not occurring. Effective organisation for meeting individual needs in the first year of school is important. It is especially important for children who are slow to move into the particular classroom programme that the school has chosen to use. By the second year at school a small number of children who need special supplementary help can easily be identified. At this time most of them can catch up to their average peers, and Reading Recovery teachers are able to guide this catching up process.

In the first three years of school, educators have their one and only chance to upset the correlation between intelligence measures and literacy progress, or between initial progress and later progress. Once an active reader and writer has constructed these literacy processes, the critical stage in the formation of a reading and writing action system will have passed.

3 Reducing reading and writing difficulties with an early intervention

Whatever their origins, reading and writing difficulties have a large learned component. It is this learned component we need to work with. We must design

- the best available lessons
- for the hardest-to-teach children
- as early as possible.

Literacy has become so important in today's technological world that slow rates of progress in beginning reading and writing in the first years of school will severely limit a child's ultimate achievements in school learning. Many alternative solutions have been proposed to overcome a slow start to literacy learning. Although most pupils make progress some fall further behind their classmates over time. Remedial treatments offered have tended to involve

- a curriculum of items (letters, sounds and words),
- derived from a list of the linguistic features of the language,
- and presented in the same prescriptive sequence for each learner.

One conclusion seems to me inescapable. The low level of success in older remedial programmes probably occurred because what is difficult about literacy learning differs markedly from child to child!

What could be achieved if some rather different supplementary instruction were available for a young learner who was clearly not able to keep up with his classmates after one year at school? Suppose the system provided, for a short period of time, an individual treatment, somewhat analogous to medical intensive care. It would occur every day and be tailored to the learner's particular needs. What if we were to

- start with whatever the individual child can do,
- design an individual series of lessons,
- allow the teacher to work with his individual strengths, whatever they were,
- build up individual areas of weakness,
- aim to have him reading books at the same level as his average peers, and,
- achieve this in the shortest possible time.

The child's progress would not be impeded by a prescriptive curriculum, and the pace of progress could be faster than in the classroom because time would not be spent on anything he could already do. If this worked he may well be able to catch up to his classmates.

The Reading Recovery early intervention was designed to accelerate literacy acquisition for most of the children falling into the lowest 20 percent of literacy learners after a year at school. It also acts as a pre-referral intervention and provides a diagnostic period of teaching to identify a small residual group of children who still need extra help and probably further specialist guidance. Reading Recovery enables an education system to deliver those two outcomes.

The intervention is based on two important hypotheses. The first is that a series of lessons for a child should be designed after a detailed observation of the ways in which that child responds to language as a written code. The teacher is concerned with how the child works on problem-solving and new learning. Attention is paid to what that child can do well and how to use these strengths to enable him to do the things he finds difficult. The learner develops many alternative ways of solving literacy problems, and increases the speed and complexity of his problem solving.

The second hypothesis is that it is economical to work with *learning to read and write* because a reciprocal relationship between these two sets of competencies allows them to support each other.

The child is not being taught a list of items but learns to select from several ways of problem-solving, to work effectively with the written language code. It is not a linguistic analysis of the language that determines the curriculum. It is an analysis of how the learner uses what he knows to go beyond his current competence and lift his level of performance. The teaching is directed to a curriculum of psychological processes (perceptual and cognitive) necessary for working with written language.

Thinking about literacy learning in this way means that we can help children who are having difficulty in different education systems (and across different languages). The problem-solving that the child learns will vary slightly from one education system to another depending on the classroom instruction that has been adopted. The competencies expected of the children by the end of their lesson series will need to differ slightly from one system to another.

My notes from P. David Pearson's address to an Ohio conference in 1999 describe Reading Recovery as distinctive in these ways:

- it increases the teaching time,
- it provides increased opportunities to engage in active cognitive processing of print,
- and it supports progress with 'on-line scaffolding of learning' on everyday printed materials.

The teachers demonstrate and coach children through ways of problem-solving texts used by readers and writers, and encourage them to make some of their thinking public. It is

- the intensity of teaching,
- the consistency of support,
- the immediacy of feedback, and
- the quality of the teaching

that makes the instruction different.

A starting point

My observations of successful children learning to read have, over the years, led to my published research reports and a view of reading acquisition expressed in the first three books listed below using the assessment tasks described in the fourth book.

> *Further reading:*
> *Becoming Literate: The construction of inner control* (1991); *By Different Paths to Common Outcomes* (1998); and *Change Over Time in Children's Literacy Development* (2001).
> *An Observation Survey of Early Literacy Achievement* (2005).

The general theory of learning to read and write described in those texts makes several assumptions.

- It assumes that a theory of reading continuous texts cannot arise from a theory of word reading. It involves problem-solving and the integration of behaviours not studied in a theory about analysing words. It must, however, explain the role of word reading and letter recognition within the theory of reading continuous text.

- It assumes that a child begins to read by attending to many different aspects of printed texts (letters, words, pictures, language, messages, stories). He will have limited knowledge and primitive early response patterns in each of these areas. Those responses change in two ways: 1) the child learns more about each of these areas, and 2) the child learns to work on the interrelationships of these areas.

- It assumes that tasks that at first require the learner's close attention gradually require less and less conscious attention (unless some local problem arises and needs to be solved). This means that what the reader is attending to and how his mind is working on the task must change over the first years of literacy learning. The beginning reader who reads quite slowly and aloud becomes the fluent, fast silent reader by about nine years of age. There are changes over time, not only in what is known, but also in how the reading or writing task is carried out.

The observation tasks provide a basis for describing what a particular child has learned about reading and writing, and to some extent, what changes are occurring in the way a reader works on texts or a writer composes and records texts.

Two distinct sets of implications for teaching can be derived from the general theory: one for classroom practice with children making successful progress in the school's chosen curriculum, and another for the children who are the lowest achievers in the age group. This second set of practices should not exclude any child in an ordinary classroom for any reason and may also contribute useful information about some children in special education.

What would a successful supplementary (pre-referral) intervention in the early years of school look like?

Individual instruction

Allowing a teacher 30 minutes of one-to-one interactions daily with a reluctant learner for 12 to 20 weeks sounds to many people like an expensive approach to the problem of reading and writing difficulties. It has proved to be economical in Reading Recovery for three reasons.

First, the successful children become both readers and writers, a double gain rarely addressed in debates about early literacy interventions, and usually overlooked by reviewers of Reading Recovery instruction.

Second, many children move through their series of lessons quickly, on average in 15 to 18 weeks. As a child completes his lesson series the teacher selects the next lowest achiever for individual assistance. A teacher working half-time could work with ten or more different children during a school year.

Third, after the early intervention lessons are completed successful children are able to move forward with their average or better classmates over the next three years although a few have needed further help. The economy for the education system lies in mounting high-quality instruction that is implemented with attention to detail and with annual recording of outcomes.

How can a switch to individual instruction be so powerful in its effects? It allows for the revolutionary changes in teaching recognised by Pearson. The lessons start with what the child can already do, and not from the requirements of a pre-selected programme sequence used in the classroom (see Tunmer and Chapman, 2003).

A critic might argue that more would be achieved if two or three children were taught in a group. But when the teacher designs each part of every lesson to target the cutting edge of an individual's learning the teacher can select crucial next learning. She wastes no time teaching what this learner already knows. This is a critical variable for Reading Recovery's success. The critic's challenge arises from a concept of learning and practice being delivered in set sequences to several children at once. This is not the practice adopted by medical intensive care specialists, nor should it be a substitute for designing individual lessons that target individual needs and lift individual progress swiftly. You could teach set sequences in individual lessons, but an early intervention aiming to achieve a fast turnaround of learners and to move them away from needing extra help would not approach the problem in that way.

When a teacher is faced with a group of children she inevitably makes compromises as she selects a next move for the group. She selects the books, identifies the difficulties, provides the explanations, and decides upon the amount of productive activity or practice, by some averaging of joint or group needs. The teaching is more or less the same for each child in the group, whether that is what an individual needs or not. One could predict that the particular 'hard parts' for some learners may never be addressed in the group.

Taking the lowest achievers individually the teacher can work with the limited response repertoire of a particular child, using what he knows as the context within which to introduce him to novel things and judging how long before she can move him to new material. When Iversen (1997) studied 'a group approach' to Reading Recovery the teachers in her research taught two children at a time, carefully matched for initial learning needs, and within about three weeks they were at different places in their learning and her teachers then taught two different lessons at the same time. (A longer allocation of time was needed to deliver these two lessons.)

Individual instruction has a particular advantage. It allows the child who does not know when his attempts are good and when they are poor to be personally reinforced by the teacher immediately, if he makes an appropriate attempt. (Pearson called this 'on-line scaffolding of learning' with 'immediacy of feedback' in his Ohio address.) The teacher's close supervision will allow her to detect an interfering or handicapping type of response when it creeps in, and to swiftly arrange for a better response to occur. She may structure the task (for example, using a masking card or a pointer), or she may record in her notes that she must somehow shift the child to some new basis for making choices between words. Throughout the 30-minute lesson the teacher's attention is tuned to the responding history of this one child. One teacher per pupil is the only practical way of working with children who have extremely different kinds of responses to the tasks of learning to read and write.

Further reading:
See Schmitt, M.C. et al., *Changing Futures: The influence of Reading Recovery in the United States* (2005).

An early intervention should select the lowest achievers, not excluding any child in the classroom. Schools have wanted to select children for the intervention who, in their judgement, would be 'able to profit from the intervention', and they have been willing to exclude some lowest-achievers from selection. But *clearly those are the children who will learn to read and write only if they get individual attention.*

When Reading Recovery teaching procedures are tried with groups the programmes are typically longer, they are less successful and they may involve unwarranted exclusion of some children. For example, extreme behaviour problems do not exclude a child from individual instruction but may lead to exclusion from a group. Or, some of the flexibility the teacher has to select books to suit a child's ethnic and language strengths is lost with a group delivery of lessons. In contrast, individually designed instruction in individually delivered lessons provides the intensive care that results in the fastest recovery of a normal trajectory of progress for any child.

A few children in early interventions make progress but are not ready to survive alone in the classroom. This diagnosis can be made after only 20 weeks, and the child can be referred early for psychological assessment and for longer-term help. Early identification of a group of children who need extended help is a positive outcome of the earlier intervention. When this early intervention was designed it was always the intention that it should contribute to the early identification of those children who would need longer-term help.

Acceleration

The child requiring help with early reading and writing has been making very slow progress and has been dropping further and further behind his classmates. In order to become an average-progress child he will have to progress faster than his classmates for a time if he is to catch up to them. Acceleration refers to this increase in the rate of progress.

To say that the slow-progress child who cannot be pushed or placed under stress should now learn at an accelerated rate seems to be a puzzling contradiction. However, I have already discussed two important factors that help this to occur. He will get one-to-one teaching and the lessons will start with his strengths and proceed according to what he is able to learn about reading and writing. He will get help but his teacher will follow his leads and his needs.

In addition, whenever possible the child will read and write text. He will not be diverted from printed texts to pictorial material or puzzles but will be taught what he needs to learn in the context of continuous text. (Rare exceptions to this could occur when a child has physical handicaps.) Any new letter or high-frequency word or a spelling pattern attended to in isolation is also used in the same lesson in text reading and text writing, and the learner interacts with the teacher about the relationships of new detail to old continuous text which he remembers.

Acceleration depends upon how well the teacher selects the clearest, easiest, most memorable examples with which to establish a new response, skill, principle or procedure. For example, the child trying to recall how to use the verb ending 'ing' may be helped by the first example of an 'ing' word that he learned. The teacher will select reading and writing opportunities that reiterate this child's new learning in the context of his learning history. She will choose clear examples of a procedure he could use. Productive examples are those that lead to further reading or writing control in a number of different ways.

With problem readers it is not enough for the teacher to have rapport, to generate interesting tasks and generally to be a good teacher. The teacher must be able to design a superbly sequenced series of lessons determined by the particular child's competencies, and make highly skilled decisions moment by moment during the lesson. The child must never engage in unnecessary activities because that wastes learning time. If the teacher judges that a child can make a small leap forward, she must watch the effects of this decision and take immediate supportive action if necessary. An expert teacher will help the child to leap appropriately; she will not walk the child through a preconceived sequence of learning step by step.

Acceleration is achieved as the child takes over the learning process and works independently, discovering new things for himself inside and outside the lessons. Therefore what the teacher attends to and how she interacts with the child changes noticeably across the lesson series. He must continually push the boundaries of his own knowledge, and not only during his lessons. The teacher must watch for and use this personal searching on the part of the child to shift the emphases in her teaching.

Achieving acceleration is not easy, but it must be constantly borne in mind. During Reading Recovery training a teacher is challenged if she seems to be wasting the learner's time, especially when her colleagues notice that she is teaching something the child has already shown that he can do!

Two kinds of learning must be kept in balance: on the one hand performing with success on familiar material strengthens the decision-making processes of the reader, and on the other hand independent problem-solving on new and interesting texts with supportive teaching extends the ability to problem-solve. The teacher chooses texts with both kinds of learning in mind: she wants to maximise the advantage of 'knowing what' and 'knowing how'. With a measured dose of opportunities she steadily lifts the level of challenge. Working with both familiar and new material contributes to acceleration.

The teacher will foster and support acceleration as she moves the child quickly through his series of lessons, making superb decisions and wasting no unnecessary time, but the teacher cannot produce or induce acceleration. The teacher cannot decide that the time has come and she will now accelerate the rate of progress. It is the learner who accelerates because some things no longer need his attention and are done more easily. Things that are familiar come together more rapidly, and allow the learner to attend to novel things. When this happens at an ever-increasing rate acceleration of learning occurs.

Daily instruction, an intensive programme

Reading Recovery lessons must occur daily. In that way even the child who cannot remember from day to day can be helped. The teacher acts as the memory of what his response was yesterday, and prompts him accordingly. (Twice-weekly lessons are a weak approach to meeting special learning needs. Twice a week with a group of children makes it impossible to design the lessons for a constantly increasing level of challenge for every individual learner.)

The power of early intervention to effect change is diminished

- if the child is not attending regularly or
- if the teacher is not available to teach (because she is ill, allocated to other duties, away on professional development courses, or relieving for a colleague).

Therefore Reading Recovery teachers must speak with parents before the lesson series begins to establish an oral contract to have the child at school. Then they must follow through on this to achieve daily attendance. In the meantime *principals must protect the teacher's daily access to her pupils in the interests of achieving the greatest progress in the minimum number of lessons.* When daily, intensive programming is not achieved the quality of the teaching and the outcomes of the intervention can be seriously affected.

The principle of delivering an intensive early intervention allows the teacher to closely record and engineer the shifts in the child's responding. Short lessons held often are important for success. This allows for learning to be carried over from one day to the next.

Getting down to detail

In learning to read the child making normal progress picks up and organises for himself a wealth of detailed information about letters, print, words and reading with a spontaneity that leads some people to believe that many things do not have to be taught. There is evidence that this attention to print in the environment, in books, and in early attempts to write begins early in the preschool years for some children who are only two or three year olds. Others, however, may have paid little attention to print in the environment.

From time to time the child who is learning to read will have to pay very close attention to the detail of print. Letter learning must be done, although the reading of simple books can begin when only a few letters are known. There will be a gradual accumulation of letter knowledge as the child reads and writes.

Which low achievers will need to attend to letter formation? This question is not about the aesthetic features of good handwriting, but it is about children who find it hard to analyse a letter's form into its parts, or cannot 'find' in their minds the routine they once learned for producing it.

Although a child knows most of the letters one cannot assume that he has access to this knowledge while reading continuous text. One of the problems often encountered is a child not seeing any relationship between letters he recognises in isolation (perhaps in one particular teaching situation) and what he is looking at in continuous text in a reading book. He has yet to learn how to use one source of knowledge in another context. And even when children selected for early intervention seem to be reading quite well, one cannot assume that letter learning will 'fall into place' as it seems to do with children making average progress. Hidden confusions will continue to affect progress.

However, when the teacher becomes too involved in teaching for detail the principle of acceleration can be seriously threatened. Undue attention to the detail of letters, for example, can block the child's ability to use his language knowledge and the meaning of the text, as part of his information base for decision-making. If the learner comes to believe that focal attention must be given to letter detail and becomes committed to doing this he may find it difficult later to shift to a higher gear and take a faster approach to the reading of text.

At times the child will need to give close attention to a particular sub-task to make sure it is learned, but must become able to perform the task later with almost no attention.

Tuition on detail will be necessary. Confusions once identified must be quickly cleared and if a prop is introduced to support initial learning, such as finger-pointing, it should be discarded as soon as possible.

If the child has to make a short sharp detour from reading continuous text to study something in isolation, what is learned should soon recur in the context of continuous text because this is what reading books and writing stories is about. A detour may help the child to pay attention to some particular aspect of print but, clearly, the detail is of limited value on its own. It must in the end be used in the service of reading or writing continuous text.

Giving attention to print detail is an essential part of a literacy repertoire, but in the management of text reading many things have to be processed without conscious attention.

Teaching sequences

Every school and classroom has some teaching sequence by which reading is presented to children. For the child who has not progressed well in that setting it will probably not be sufficient to change to a different teacher, different material or a different approach to instruction. These remedies are often suggested, but I have not found them sufficient.

Failing children differ more among themselves in response to curriculum than average children. They are a heterogeneous group whose strengths and weaknesses are different and whose confusions and tangles may need quite different approaches from those used in the classroom. Teaching sequences of a standard kind are unlikely to meet the needs of struggling readers. While a commercial kit may be a slight improvement on nothing, the ideal lesson series will have activities individually selected to meet the needs of a particular child.

Therefore, the early intervention teacher must know of many ways to foster literacy skills, must vary her teaching sequences, and be bold in negotiating short-cuts. To be able to pick and choose among teaching techniques and learning activities, and pull the right one into her lesson at the crucial moment, that teacher must be very familiar with possible teaching alternatives.

An experienced classroom teacher brings a great deal of knowledge to her training for early intervention work because she is aware of the progressions made by children in classrooms and the variations among learners in a classroom. She will have to free herself from set sequences and vary her teaching to meet the particular needs of hard-to-teach individuals, and she has to select the direction that will suit a particular child. It is important for her to be articulate about how the average children in the classroom read and write. She must bring her individual children by different routes to work like those average children. That is the endpoint of her intervention.

Most schools adopt a published series of books as the gradient of difficulty through which their children progress, and they refer to children's progress levels in terms of such books. In other programmes children read story books, graded roughly for difficulty, and progress is assessed by some other means, such as a standardised test or an informal prose inventory on a graded set of text material.

An early intervention teacher wishing to bring her students to the levels of achievement of their average classmates will also need to have some sequence of difficulty through which she attempts to move her students. In Reading Recovery teachers use many different books but an attempt is made to grade these simple story books against some benchmark series. A book may be selected because it can contribute to a particular child's learning problem of the moment but the teacher knows how the level of that book can be equated to the benchmark series.

The instruction needs to be related in some way to the progressions in the reading series used in the classrooms but it need not take place on that series of books. Early intervention teachers may keep a child on one level of difficulty for a short period. They will have the child read several new books of parallel difficulty until the child is ready to take the next lift or challenge. Occasionally the teacher may take a carefully calculated risk and support the child to jump forward two levels. Despite the child's initial uncertainty she will hopefully be able to conclude that the acceleration was justified. In both these cases the child would not usually be reading the graded material of the classroom series but material known to be of equivalent difficulty (see Clay, 2005).

Reciprocal gains of reading and writing

The child who has failed to learn to read is usually also struggling to write stories. Early *reading* interventions often exclude the teaching of writing. This is unacceptable. Writing is treated as some kind of extension that comes after reading or as a different subject. Educators separate them in timetables and curricula. An alternative view sees both reading and writing in the early acquisition stage as contributing to learning about print. Learning to write letters, words and sentences is particularly helpful as the child learns to make the visual discriminations of detail in print that he will use in his reading (Clay, 1998, 2001).

While the child has only limited control in writing and in reading he can be encouraged to search for information in his memories of either reading or writing, establishing reciprocity between these aspects of learning about printed language.

In Reading Recovery children write messages every day. It is in the writing part of the daily lesson that children are required to pay attention to letter detail, a sequence of phonemes, a sequence of letters, and the links between messages in oral language and messages in printed language. One thing is particularly important. Children must learn to hear the sounds in words they want to write and find appropriate ways to write those sounds down. The writing knowledge serves as a resource of information that can help the reader. However, this reciprocity does not occur spontaneously. The teacher must remember to direct the child to use what he knows in reading when he is writing and vice versa.

Reading Recovery's research shows that as the child comes to control a writing vocabulary of 40 or more words (*his words, not a required set*) he comes to use strategies for spelling more and more words in his language. Reading and writing are interwoven throughout the Reading Recovery lesson series and teaching proceeds on the assumption that both provide learned responses that facilitate new responding in either area. The reciprocity of learning in reading and writing is something the children learn to utilise in some implicit way.

The simple messages, stories or sentences that Reading Recovery children write are viewed critically by some educators. They want these children to run before they can crawl, to perhaps compose a larger story across several weeks of lessons. Daily writing shared with the teacher on simple messages helps these children to understand more about the task, to learn to compose (simple though the composition may be), and to emerge from their lesson series with great resources for making the most of the writing opportunities in the classroom.

Reading knowledge tends to draw ahead of writing knowledge after a while, but at the beginning of school what the child can write is a good indicator of what the child knows in detail about written language. When a child leaves an early intervention the prediction is made that the child is likely to survive in the classroom continuing to increase his level of performance (though not, of course, at the accelerated rate achieved in daily individual lessons). That prediction is safer if the child has satisfactory levels of performance in both reading and writing, and longitudinal research evidence shows that the prediction is more at risk if the writing has been neglected, and allowed to lag behind reading progress! (Clay and Tuck, 1993)

4 The shape of the child's series of lessons in Reading Recovery

Do you know how reading is being taught in your school? You probably know what curriculum or curriculum guidelines you use but do you know what reading processes are actually being developed by the particular curriculum that is used in your school? What are the children who are successful learning to do, and what have the children who do not succeed learned to do? (They may have learned things which are blocking their progress.) Descriptions of what children are actually learning should differ somewhat from school to school because your school entrants may have had very different preschool experiences from those of children in another school.

> *Further reading:*
> See *An Observation Survey of Early Literacy Achievement* (2005),
> pp. 140–41 for discussion of how to get this kind of information
> on a school's instructional programme.

This is important information for schools to have if they want to identify the group of children in the school who have particular difficulty with literacy learning. *Every reading programme has its 'risk areas'.* Every reading programme stresses some facets of the reading process and as a consequence gives less attention to other facets. To reassure people we talk about a 'balanced' classroom programme but we rarely specify in detail what that means.

The teacher in early intervention must help her students to gain the same competencies as the successful children in the school and to achieve at the same level, so she needs to know how the successful children in her school work on the literacy tasks of their classrooms. *Sensitive observation of the children making slow progress must take into account what is being learned by the children making satisfactory progress in classrooms.*

Having clear descriptions of the day-to-day teaching and the sequential progressions of the school's programme will help the early intervention teacher to make better decisions about when to begin and when to discontinue a series of special lessons for a particular child. Early literacy intervention does not need an elaborate definition of reading difficulties. One simply takes the pupil from wherever he is, however limited his achievements are, and lifts his performance to somewhere appropriate for progressing well with *his* particular teacher, in *his* particular class, in *his* school.

Three things are taken for granted.

- The first is that the child will be part of an ongoing classroom programme while he receives this extra tuition.

- The second is that the extra tutoring will be designed to suit the individual learner, will be delivered daily, and will be limited in time to a maximum of 20 weeks before further appraisal is made of his most facilitative educational placement.

- The third is that the teacher will understand *a theory of what the child must learn to attend to and how he must work with print as he reads and writes.* She will also be able to design a series of lessons within the framework of that theory that will vary from child to child so that the diversity of the lowest achievers in the age group will be addressed.

The recommendations that follow apply specifically to efficient and effective operation of a Reading Recovery intervention designed to minimise literacy learning difficulties.

First encounters with a written code for language

A major challenge for the young child entering formal instruction is finding out what the marks on the paper stand for. A code is many things — laws, regulations, a set of rules, a cipher, a secret language, signals or sign-system. To the novice, print and writing are a set of signs that adults seem to understand. Initially the marks have no sound. Very slowly as preschool children explore the shapes of printed forms they come to understand that they have something to do with the language they speak. In fact when something is written down in print, different adults can tell you what it says! Children also learn a basic concept, that print stands for something, usually through learning the names of people or pets or toys. They have yet to find out how this all works.

When children start school their code knowledge will range from nothing to very informed. New things are learned quite rapidly in a good school programme but a few children will begin school with limited literacy knowledge. Each child will know different things. These individual differences result from preschool experiences that have been different. To quote one individual case, from Glenda Bissex (1980):

> At 5:6 Paul demonstrated his ability to decode with no context cues simple words like baby, stop, yes, duck, join. He (deliberately) avoided continuous text.

Further reading:
Glenda Bissex wrote a book about her son's early literacy progress you might enjoy reading, called *GNYS AT WRK: A child learns to write and read* (1980).

Predictions of progress

Complete an Observation Survey for each child and write up an Observation Survey Summary Statement of the child's literacy competencies (see Part Two, Appendix, pp. 188–89). This will provide guidance about where to begin planning that child's lessons. To complete the initial design of the work this child will need to do, it is necessary for the teacher to make some predictions about the progress that this particular child will need to make.

Making 'predictions of progress' for a particular child will help the teacher maintain a long-term perspective on her day-to-day decisions. This is important. Specify the programme goals for each child. Some teachers think that the final outcome is the same for all children but that is not true. Children in the average band of readers in a classroom do not all process information in the same ways.

Although you may think that the final outcome of your lesson series might look similar for all your children, the paths to those outcomes will be different because of their individual strengths and weaknesses.

Look at what a particular child can do now and think about what he needs to learn to do. Consider the changes you would expect to see in the reading and writing behaviour of each child as he becomes a more competent reader and writer. Predict the paths of progress for each of the children entering your programme and describe the changes you expect to see in terms of each child's particular strengths and particular weaknesses.

Look at each Observation Survey Summary Sheet, *consider the profile of scores*, and look at the information used and information neglected. What are the useful things this child can do and what areas are most problematic for him? Think how this child's lesson series might have to be different from that of another child you have taught.

The predictions about this child's progress should relate what he can and cannot do on entry to the outcomes you want to see at the end of the lesson series. Put his current limitations and what he finds difficult into an account of the path you think he might need to take.

- At the end of the lesson series he will need to know how to do this and that in order to …

- and in the next few weeks he will need to know how to …

- and extra work will be needed on …

- and I will need to pay special attention to …

Record these predictions on a separate piece of paper and attach this to the Observation Survey Summary Statement. Evaluate a child's progress regularly against these predictions. Week by week you may need to adjust your predictions as new strengths and weaknesses emerge, finding space on your lesson record to note these shifts. The predictions are hypotheses about the paths children could take and children will surprise us from time to time and prove some of our first assumptions to be quite wrong. That is to be expected. Adjust or change your early predictions as you review the progress children are making.

Should trained teachers continue to write long-term predictions as well as short-term goals? Yes, I think it is a necessary part of designing a programme for each individual child based on his past history and maximising his chances of success. The first weeks of lessons lay the foundation for subsequent success. Predictions of progress ensure that teachers are crafting the instruction to suit the entry characteristics of individual children and not just proceeding down a standard path of 'things I expect children to learn'.

Roaming around the known

For the first two weeks of the lesson series stay with what the child already knows how to do. Do not deliberately teach him any new items or processes (although he will probably learn quite a lot from your task-sharing over these first ten sessions). The teaching should not start where the teacher is but where the child is! Confidence, ease, flexibility and, with luck, discovery are the keynotes of this period which I have called 'Roaming around the known'.

There are a number of reasons why 'Roaming around the known' makes a good starting point for the child's early literacy learning.

- The child and the teacher have an opportunity to get to know each other and to develop useful ways of interacting.

- The observation tasks that were used for assessment could only sample some behaviours and roaming around the known gives the teacher an opportunity to observe more of the child's ways of responding.

- The child may discover things he did not know he knew and, free of formal demands to learn, he may observe new relationships.

- The teacher is free to observe the child without the need to record all that occurs or to think particularly of her next teaching move, although making notes is necessary.

- The teacher works mostly with reading texts and writing texts. This seems to give the child the feeling that he is 'really reading and writing'.

- The teacher tries to strengthen all that the child is able to do, helping him achieve a level of confidence and fluency that will assist him later, when he moves into new learning.

- At the end of the period the child will feel comfortable with a small body of knowledge and confident to use this as a springboard for trying new things when the instruction starts. This is a firm foundation on which to build.

- The teacher can demonstrate as she reads and writes, commenting on print layout, where to start, which way to move, and how to get helpful information from a page of print. Clear demonstration is more effective than talking about these directional things.
- However, the most important reason for 'Roaming around the known' is that it requires the teacher to stop teaching from her preconceived ideas. She has to work in ways that will suit each child, working with what he is able to do. This will be her focus throughout the lesson series.

If a teacher feels impatient and wishes to get on with teaching the child 'the things she needs to put into his head' then she has not accepted that the child has to gear up to actively using his eyes, and his ears, and his thinking. He needs to take ownership of part of the tasks during this period, to feel confident to do things, and to know that the teacher will support his efforts.

Note that if a child enters Reading Recovery with higher scores on the Observation Survey tasks that child will still need to spend time roaming around the known. There will be a much wider range of literacy behaviours to explore, more confusions, and also hidden problems. It is imperative that the teacher uncover any unhelpful assumptions or unwanted habits that the child has already learned in school.

Think about the child's responses

Use these first two weeks to find out how the child responds in a teaching relationship. Time spent 'in the known' will probably not look like a typical tutoring lesson because in order to stay with what is known the teacher will share more of the tasks, repeat activities more often, intersperse reading and writing activities throughout the lesson and create ingenious innovations.

The formal lesson record is unsuitable for 'Roaming around the known'. Teachers should keep a daily diary of useful notes for themselves of what happens during these two weeks. This is not an invitation for someone to design a form. To ensure that 'Roaming around the known' is approached with an open mind, no forms should be used.

Ensure that your diary is not merely a record of the activities you create. Try to capture as many aspects of the child's behaviours as you can. Make yourself specify just how he responds. Put it into words. What does he do well? How does he help himself? What more have you noticed about the letters, words and other features of print that he knows? Did he surprise you?

Listen to the child's use of language. What is the longest utterance you have heard him construct? Write it down.

Watch for and record new evidence that did not show up on the assessment tasks of what he knows and knows how to do. Note down your insights from what he says and does, capturing what he controls well and how his control over aspects of the tasks changes as he gains more confidence.

Engage in conversation

Just as a listener tunes into a speaker, so a teacher must observe, listen to and tune into a learner. Being sensitive to the learner's thinking allows the teacher to draw the child's attention to many things. The teacher in conversation with the child creates opportunities for the child to talk, and to talk more. Any child with limited language skills needs more opportunities to talk. And the teacher provides examples of how to use language in every utterance she makes.

Throughout all lessons, not only these early ones, the conversational exchanges should be a very valuable context within which literacy learning becomes the focus.

> *Further reading:*
> See *By Different Paths to Common Outcomes*, chapters 1 and 2, pp. 5–36.

Build fluency on the very little he knows

Aim to bring the child to confidence and flexibility with the things that he knows. Design interesting, shared activities and have the child contribute what you know he knows as his share of the activity. Go over what he knows in many different ways in each lesson. Praise him for his efforts. Show delight in everything he does, however minor.

The Observation Survey will have shown up some of the things that the child can do, and if you share tasks and ask him to participate when you are sure he will be successful, you can engage in some new activities that will catch his attention. Draw him in to sharing these activities.

The child needs to feel in control of what you ask him to do, as this child did when he told his mother,

> I can't read but I can read her books!

Being in control is important at every level of achievement throughout the lesson series.

Hold his interest, bolster his confidence, make him your co-worker. Get the responding fluent and habituated but even at this stage encourage flexibility, using the same knowledge in different ways. Work until your ingenuity runs out and until he is moving fluently around his personal corpus of responses — the letters, the words and the messages he knows how to read or write.

Be sure the foundation is firm and the child confident. Both the child and the teacher should be straining at the leash and wanting to go further but the teacher should resist the temptation to begin teaching too soon. Children who have not made a strong start with literacy learning need this two-week period before the teacher introduces them to new learning.

It will be great if he notices things on his own but you may need to prompt him to recognise the things you know he knows in different settings. Listen carefully to what he says and the connections he is making. Be prepared to be surprised by his ingenuity!

If you have caught the child's attention he will, of course, notice, learn from, and soon want to engage in, some of the things he sees you do! Allow him space and scope to do this. He needs to be able to find what he already knows being used here and there in all kinds of different settings. It is very important in early learning for the learner to discover something he knows in different settings or contexts. Try to arrange for the newest things to recur in different parts of every session. This will help him to gain greater control over what he knows how to do.

Encourage his participation in reading

Use readable texts. You will have found several appropriate texts that the child can read at 90 percent accuracy or better as part of the Observation Survey. The following are suggestions to help you in the search for other books this child can read. They get easier as you go down the list:

- a very easy story book
- a very simple story you have read to this child
- a simple book about an experience the child has had
- a simple story you write for the child keeping to his known vocabulary
- a simple text he has dictated.

Each of these is moving one step closer to the child's limited resources. The better he is the further up the sequence you can start. The weaker he is the lower down that sequence you should start. You cannot rely on a published sequence of material for these earliest lessons. The teacher must be the expert who chooses and sequences the texts for a Reading Recovery pupil — this is critical.

Further reading:
See *An Observation Survey of Early Literacy Achievement* (2005), pp. 32–33.

Of course reading to children can be part of 'Roaming around the known'. You can use it as a setting for rediscovering those things he knows, and if you make some of 'his own books' at this time you will be able to incorporate what he knows in a deliberate way. You can also read many simple trade storybooks to the child, making the simplest texts sound exciting (like *Where's Spot?* and *Cat on the Mat*). Your phrasing and intonation will make the story sound good. The child may want to join in or even take over when you have read a book more than once.

Aim to have the child feel in control of some activities.

Encourage his participation in writing

In each session create many different kinds of opportunities for talking about a variety of things. Choose what you know will interest him.

Make up stories with him about things that catch his interest and you be the scribe who writes them down, always allowing the child to write anything that he knows. He needs to feel in control of what he can do as did this child, who said petulantly to his teacher,

> I wanted to do that 'I'!

Encourage him as he writes the things that recur in the different messages you are writing with him. Stress fluency from the beginning, and encourage him to write something he knows more quickly. Use a variety of different media to write with and write on.

Reread these stories to him. This will help him understand that from ideas, stories are constructed that can be written and read. He may want to read with you, or even try to read it himself.

As you engage in writing activities you may be able to add to the information from the Observation Survey because you find out more about what he can write unaided. At all times keep a record in your diary of what you discover that he can do.

New behaviours may appear

You will probably notice some things emerging that you did not think the child knew. Useful new behaviours appear as he begins to relate things one to another. He remembers a book with this or that in it. A letter reminds him of a classmate's name. He reads 'car' for 'are' or some other mismatch that makes you feel he is getting closer to effective decisions.

There will be reasons for the appearance of new behaviours. A child can solve problems in many alternative ways in his daily life. He uses what he knows, he does what he knows how to do, and he jumps to a solution. He begins to apply this strategic problem-solving that he learnt in everyday life to his work with his teacher.

Why didn't he do this before? When one is having difficulty with a task one tries several approaches. When an attempt results in failure one ceases to try it. The struggling reader and writer has stopped trying to problem-solve because he could not be successful. If you give him your support and he succeeds then he begins to try again to use some of the old discarded strategic activities. Once he is doing this he can discover new things that work. You should show delight when he spontaneously relates this to that. Often what

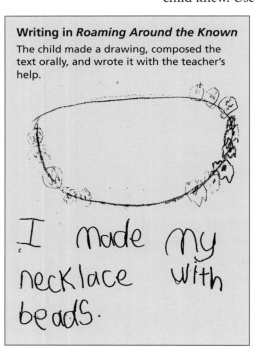

Writing in *Roaming Around the Known*
The child made a drawing, composed the text orally, and wrote it with the teacher's help.

I made my necklace with beads.

he discovers was not one of the things you were looking for. You could easily miss how clever he was!

So you unleash two sets of responses — those discarded approaches this child has ceased to use on texts, and new ones that come from 'we know not where'. You probably could not achieve this if you were trying to use a standard or published curriculum. You are likely to be successful because you are responding to the child in an individual teaching situation. It only works this way if the child's own competencies are for the most part determining the teacher's design for his lesson series.

Moving into instruction: shift the responsibility for learning to the child

Once you move out of 'Roaming around the known' and into the lesson framework you need to make clear 'Lesson Records' of how the child responds to your scaffolding of the tasks in each lesson. These records inform your planning and assist you in making the best teaching decisions. It is important to begin with the first lesson and to gradually get used to recording a brief note about what you did and how the child responded as it happens so that later you can return and complete the detail on your records. Teaching is the most important role and should take precedence over recording during lessons. Forms are provided in the Appendices in Part Two with reading activities on one side and writing activities on the other. A comments column is provided for you to evaluate your teaching decisions when you reflect, later on, on the lesson.

A typical tutoring session

In Reading Recovery a typical tutoring session would include each of these activities, usually in the following order, as the format of the daily lesson:

• reading two or more familiar books	text
• rereading yesterday's new book and taking a running record	text
• working with letter identification	letters and words
• breaking words into parts	letters and clusters
• writing a story	word work and text
• hearing and recording sounds	sounds
• reconstructing the cut-up story	text
• listening to the new book introduction	text
• attempting to read the new book	text

There are several reasons for placing the new book at the end of the lesson, although some teachers have argued that the child is tired by this stage. The main reason is that each previous activity has encouraged the child to work on his own problems and to actively engage in solving problems.

By the end of the lesson he should have revised easy reading, letter knowledge, links between letters and sounds, and his monitoring strategies in the cut-up story, and he should tackle his new book with his repertoire of responses in their most accessible form: they were used recently! The teacher will have carefully considered the challenges of the new text when choosing it and will have been aware of these during earlier lesson activities. Individual variations in the lesson format are always possible, providing there is a sound rationale based on a particular child's response to lessons.

A second reason is that some new learning and/or rehearsal of a processing behaviour for text reading, like a systematic left-to-right approach to lines, or to letters in a word, can be practised during the other segments of the lesson.

A third reason for this placement of the new book is that there will be a minimum of interference between this timing and the rereading of the book the next day.

Introducing new material

At this stage there are some useful guidelines that help to keep the task easy.

- Make sure the child can *hear* a distinction or difference between two sounds or two words before you try to teach him to see the difference. Don't assume he can hear it.

- Start with large units, not the smallest ones, then separate some words out of phrases (heard or seen) or separate sounds or letters out of words.

- Encourage the use of hand and eye together. The use of the eyes alone comes later in the learning sequence.

- Link something the child does easily with something he finds hard (for support) before asking for the difficult response on its own.

- Teach most new things by demonstrating slowly. Prompting helps when the child is more competent. Question the child when you need to understand what he is doing.

- Teaching all the items in a category is a teacher's hang-up. What the child needs to know is two or three similar items and some strategies for recognising new related examples as he reads more texts.

> *Further reading:*
> Steven Pinker discussed this in *Words and Rules* (2000) in a chapter called 'Kids say the darndest things'. See also Part Two, pp. 137–38).

Prompts and prompting

What are prompts? Let us assume that the child is making a decision about what the next word in a text could be. There are several kinds of information he could use. The teacher asks herself 'What is the most facilitating thing I can call for (for this child)?'

- She may indicate where he should be attending.

- She may prompt him to locate something useful.

- She may direct his attention to text meaning or to language structure or to letter-sound information, because this is something he knows.

- She may prompt for another reason related to fine-tuning of the information-processing system. She may be able to tell that the child is using some types of information but is overlooking something else. In this case the teacher will prompt the child to remember to use information he is ignoring.

- Sometimes the teacher will prompt to interrupt or break into an old habit that is a problem to this reader. The teacher in this case intends to break the link to the unwanted response.

The child can only generate a novel response from things he knows very, very well. If you expect him to get 'stop' from 'hop' then the word 'hop' has to be very familiar. A prompt is a call for action to do something within his control.

Prompts are not just talk. How you prompt depends upon where this child is at this point of this text, and what else needs to be integrated into his reading processing. The prompt should send the child in search of a response in his network of responses.

Too much prompting interferes with the development of independent solving.

Confusions

Now turn to the child's confusions. Without increasing the difficulty level and staying mostly with text reading, record and think about this particular child's confusions. Plan an attack on them. Talk to another couple of teachers about the easiest way to go from where the child is to less confusion. That way you will find out what a blinkered approach each of us has to these difficulties and to teaching sequences. Probably you and your colleagues will not agree. Never mind. You have added the colleague's hypotheses to your own and can now approach the child's confusions tentatively, and with an open mind. In Reading Recovery do not rely on your own hunches. Be objective and critical of your own assumptions. Consult colleagues and Tutors or Teacher Leaders.

Some pointers about confusions are these.

- Don't present them side by side. Get Item A well established and known for several weeks before you bring back Item B. This applies to confusing letters, confusing sounds, and confusing words.

- Don't teach by the least noticeable difference principle. It is easier to learn gross distinctions first and gradually to make finer and finer distinctions.

- Is the child's difficulty in seeing a difference? If so, have him dictate, write, cut up, and reassemble texts.

- Is the child's difficulty in hearing a difference? If so, articulate it for him and with him very slowly, and teach him to do this for himself.

- Is the child's difficulty with order or sequence (left to right)? (Sequence refers to the sequence of letters in a word, words in a sentence, sentences on a page, or ideas in a story.) Have the child dictate a sentence for the teacher to write, then teacher and child can share these tasks — read it, cut it up, reassemble it, and write it.

If you have to shift from texts into items or other details at any point to help the child learn something, remember to make this a *necessary but temporary detour*. Plan to return to the same teaching point while the child is reading text, preferably within the same lesson, and/or several times within the next four days.

There is a general principle involved here. Usually when the child has a confusion he is dealing with a package of information bound together — he is not distinguishing seeing print, from hearing words, from order and sequence issues. Teachers often confuse learners when they also work on the 'package' and do not help the child separate out the parts of the 'package' clearly in their conversations — the look, the sounds of the spoken word, the order of the letters, or the sequence of words.

Building the foundations for a self-extending system

Teachers aim to produce independent readers so that reading and writing improve whenever children read and write. The reader who problem-solves independently has continual access to new learning. Some things become routine and the brain takes over most of the checking and rapidly locates familiar things. The reader is then free to deliberately attend to other things and can, independent of the teacher, extend his own learning.

On text of appropriate level of difficulty the child can

- monitor his own reading and writing,
- search for information in word and letter sequences, and in meanings,
- discover new things for himself,
- cross-check one source of information with another,
- repeat as if to confirm his reading or writing so far,
- and self-correct to solve the problem. (See also Part One, p. 52.)

Teachers can help children to work in these ways from their earliest attempts to read and write. They can work at monitoring, searching, discovering, cross-checking and repeating on easy texts to which they are introduced. They can detect when things do not match with their past experience, and they can succeed in correcting themselves, and learn to solve new words without the teacher's help. These early strategic activities begin to work together 'in integrated ways'. Children become able to select an activity to solve a particular problem.

As the child reaches out to read more complex texts and writes longer and more involved stories these operations are used with increasing speed and fluency on

- longer stretches of meaning
- less familiar language
- less predictable texts.

Ken Goodman and Carolyn Burke in 1973 wrote that the proficient reader gets the most meaning with the least effort in the fastest time!

He needs to be able to solve multisyllabic words within more difficult texts using clusters of letters and working quickly. The ways in which the child solves the challenges of seeing and solving words sequentially across a sentence put him in touch with new words, new structures, new styles, or genres. They provide the reader and writer with a tremendous quantity of practice for his known vocabularies (used in speaking, in writing, and in reading). The child is extending his own literacy learning and is building his own neural networks to support continuing progress.

Encourage the beginnings of a self-extending system early. The child is learning how to read *because of the effective processing he does when he reads*. Using what he can do well makes a good system stronger. Contrast this with forcing a child to use a confused processing system without offering help. That can only create further confusion!

- Give the child ways to detect error for himself.
- Encourage attempts to correct error.
- Give him clues to aid self-correction.
- Allow him to make checks or repetitions to confirm his first attempts.
- When he works out a word or text for himself ask him 'How did you know?' Do not overdo this. It is not something that a good reader does, but teachers do it occasionally because it can help them to help the child. (See Part Two, pp. 171–72.)

Teachers engage in these activities to foster the development of independent problem-solving:

- prompting constructive activity
- working with new knowledge

- accepting the child's initiatives
- accepting partially correct responses
- playing with anticipation
- developing attention to features
- asking the child 'to learn'
- praising the way a child worked towards the solution, whether it was reached or not
- lifting the difficulty level
- revisiting the familiar.

Further reading:
A reference for that list is Clay (1998), 'Introducing storybooks to young readers' in *By Different Paths to Common Outcomes*, pp. 171–84.

Increasing text difficulty

Cautiously increase the text difficulty and repeat the things listed above. Give massive practice on texts at this next level if necessary before you increase the difficulty level again.

Now look at what he cannot do

If the child is to move into higher-level texts then the teacher must recognise that the reader will need to have many different ways to approach print. She must encourage him to be flexible, and to try a variety of approaches. She must pay particular attention to what she thinks would have the greatest payoff.

Some ways to do this for a particular child are:

- practise fast oral recall of familiar objects
  - say all the words you know around a theme,
  - name four things on the table,
  - point to five things and talk about their size (big chair, tiny insect, and so on)
  - find two words that are alike, the teacher adds another, and the child thinks of a fourth;
- or practise anticipating what kinds of sentence structures could follow what has already been read;
- or hear sound sequences, first and last sounds, clusters of sounds, and hard-to-hear sounds buried in the middle of some words;
- or learn how to listen to and work with syllables and chunks;

- or practise identifying letters and clusters faster, and finding letters and letter patterns in print.

Introduce one of these invitations like a turn in a natural conversation and, if it seems helpful, repeat it for a couple of days.

Get two colleagues together and listen to their ideas about priorities for this child and how they would achieve them. That exposes your assumptions to critical analysis. Keep in mind that the teacher at all times must decide the next most powerful strategic activity that could help this particular child to increase his processing of information in text.

Now go back to your pupil and ask him what he would like to learn next. Try to work this in with your priorities.

Fast perceptual processing

Everything we do in mature reading and writing will rely on fast accurate perception of language sounds (captured by the ears) and visual symbols (captured by the eyes) as we read and write. You cannot write with pen or keyboard without fast visual feedback on what you have done so far.

The preschooler who works with print for the first time in reading or writing will also approach the task with the fast perceptual processing he uses in his environment and will not pick up the detail of print.

He has to slow down while he learns to make detailed distinctions and then speed up again to fast processing that includes all the new detail he has learned. How to pay attention to detail in a slow, careful manner is learned from the teacher, but as soon as the detail is easily recognised the teacher should lead the learner back to fast processing. Too often teaching practice perpetuates slow processing. Readers do need to analyse and solve problems but they also have to work fast.

- Involving the hand (finger-pointing, tracing, writing, using magnetic letters) encourages attention to detail, but the hand is too slow to be part of skilled reading. Using the hand for too long can impede fast perceptual processing.

- If the teacher guides the learner through an activity, her talk or demonstrations will be slow and necessary but the competent reader needs to work fast.

- Talking yourself through a movement or analysis (letting your words guide your actions) is a way to slow down attending (when necessary) but this gets in the way of fast perception of letters and words.

The progress of a child in early intervention depends on the astute judgement of the teacher about when to slow up and attend to detail and how soon to call for quick responding to letters, words, and print features that are known. What you know must be processed fast.

Some organisational points

Teachers have to keep all those slow analytic processes going on new text but arrange for massive opportunity for this child to read enchantingly interesting texts, of just the right difficulty level, fluently. They can vary the type of text to foster flexibility. They can change authors and change genres. They can be conservative about recommending an end to supplementary help but work hard to make the reader and writer as independent as possible.

Developing effective strategic activities

Reading Recovery procedures have sometimes been questioned because they appear to require correct responding from children. This is not true.

There is a particular opportunity for revision and reworking in the one-to-one teaching situation. Child and teacher are talking about the reading or the writing as it occurs. There is opportunity for the child to initiate dialogue about his response as he works and for the teacher to help in many different ways. However, Reading Recovery sets the highest value on independent responding, and this must involve the risks of being wrong. Children should gain some measure of independence on their tasks at each book level, even those who are novice readers.

> *Further reading:*
> See *An Observation Survey of Early Literacy Achievement* (2005), p. 22, and *Becoming Literate: The construction of inner control*, pp. 199, 295–96; and *By Different Paths to Common Outcomes*, p. 171.

What the teacher will do is to set some priorities as to which kinds of new learning she will attend to — just one or two things — and let the other behaviours that were incorrect go unattended for the moment.

The goal of the teaching is to assist the child to construct effective networks in his brain for linking up all the strategic activity that will be needed to work on texts, not merely to accumulate items of knowledge. It is necessary to develop self-correcting by allowing room for self-correcting to be initiated by the child. A teacher who allowed only for correct responding would not be allowing the child to explore the strategy-strengthening potentials of self-correcting behaviours!

Any theoretical position that includes self-monitoring and self-correcting as significant behaviour in reading or in writing implies the existence of near misses, approximations, uncorrected responses and sometimes corrected responses. The important thing about the self-corrections is that the child initiates them because he decides that something is wrong and calls up his own resources for working on a solution.

An example of reading book progress

Rochelle had almost a full series of lessons but may have been discontinued at too low a level. She made steady progress in the following year but three years later her progress was slower than average. She had 17 weeks in tutoring and only 41 lessons (so obviously that was not a daily programme). She could have been continued for a further three weeks.

Rochelle entered the programme at Level 1 (New Zealand Ministry of Education 'Ready to Read' books, 1963) and at that time was just beginning to recognise words in a text. *She read 22 early little books* before she began her climb up through the reading levels. At each level she read several storybooks. Her teacher usually only recorded her accuracy on the 'benchmark' books, the 'Ready to Read' books, and those are what are recorded in the table below. The teacher's choice of books and her timing of the increase in difficulty level show excellent judgement and good pacing of her pupil.

ROCHELLE'S PROGRESS: BOOKS READ, BOOK LEVEL AND DIFFICULTY LEVEL				
Week of programme	Title		How difficult* was the book for the child	Equivalent 'Ready to Read' Book Level
1–4	(22 Titles)[1]		(No accuracy records)	
5	Cuckoo In The Nest	(PM)	Easy	3
5	Merry-Go-Round (plus 1 title)	(PM)	Easy	3
7	The Fire Engine (plus 1 title)	(R-to-R)	Easy	5
7	Planes (plus 1 title)	(PM)	Easy	5
8	The Escalator	(Star)	Easy	6
8	Going To School	(R-to-R)	Instructional	7
10	Playtime	(R-to-R)	Easy	8
10	Christmas Shopping (plus 1 title)	(R-to-R)	Easy	9
10	Saturday Morning (plus 2 titles)	(R-to-R)	Easy	10
11	The Christmas Tree (plus 1 title)	(PM)	Easy	11
11	Painting The Shed	(R-to-R)	Easy	11
12	A Country School (plus 1 title)	(R-to-R)	Easy	12
13	The Pet Show (plus 1 title)	(R-to-R)	Easy	13
14	At The Camp (plus 1 title)	(R-to-R)	—	—
16	A Wet Morning (plus 1 title)	(PM)	Instructional	14
16	The Little Red Bus	(PM)	Instructional	13
16	The Pets Run Away (plus 4 titles)	(Playtime)	Instructional	14

* Easy: 95–100% accuracy achieved   Instructional: 90–94% accuracy achieved   Hard: below 90% accuracy

1 This refers to other books read but not named here.

However, the overall pattern of her progress makes one wonder about several things.

- Was her school attendance a continuing problem?
- Was her writing behaviour not taken to a high level?
- When her lessons were discontinued were her competencies satisfactory for the average group in her classroom?
- Might her progress in the classroom in her fourth and subsequent school years be under threat?

Reading Recovery teachers have to make complex decisions when they recommend that a child's series of lessons be discontinued.

Rochelle's pattern of progress should not be taken as a model. Each child's selection of books, rate of progress, starting and finishing points will be different. All that Rochelle's record demonstrates is how the shape of a Reading Recovery lesson series worked out for one child.

5 How children's behaviours change during a series of individual lessons

An environment for learning

In the first two weeks the teacher in early intervention creates the environment for the series of individual lessons she is designing for a particular child. The environment includes the context, the teacher's assumptions and expectations, the model she provides of a reader and a writer, and her awareness of novice-expert differences.

The path along which the child has come to you will have been individual and unusual. He may have had a few helpful opportunities to learn key things. You could just offer him opportunities to learn and observe carefully how he engages with them. You do not need to assume that he has to discover these things alone. We can share the tasks of reading and writing by doing for the child what he cannot do for himself. That provides him with a model of doing — of how to carry out the task — and leaves him with the feeling there is more to learn. (See Dyson, 1990.)

Teachers adjust their expectations

If there is any description of progressions in literacy learning it belongs not in the activities, not in a curriculum sequence, but in the heads of teachers, and it guides their every interaction with a learner or a group of learners. Whether the activity helps or hinders children's learning depends on the tentativeness and reflective practice of teachers who know how to open doors to learning and recognise when a door is beginning to close for a particular child.

Much discussion about instruction has been directed to getting correct performance, as if learning to read depended on an accumulation of correct responses. However, many of the child's early attempts to read are partially right and partially wrong, and, like parents talking to a little child, teachers need to make a facilitating response to the half-right, half-wrong response of the child at a particular moment in time. They must respond to gradual shifts in less than perfect performance. (A good analogy is with the less than perfect language of the two-year-old which gradually shifts to the control of the four- or five-year-old.) The child passes this particular point in his experience only once. What does the teacher have to know or do to make the most of it?

When children are novice readers their cognitive processes used for reading are being formed, undergoing changes from less expert to more expert. Available theory rarely addresses this problem. Yet that is what reading is at the acquisition stage. Sensitive and systematic observation of behaviour is really the only way to monitor gradual shifts across imperfect responding (and research in oral language acquisition has demonstrated this).

Changes teachers might observe during lessons

In an earlier guidebook published in 1993 there was a table of some changes that seem to occur. I did not emphasise then the need for teachers to adjust their expectations and interactions during the lesson series according to the progress of each learner.

So to encourage teachers to think about the changes they need to make in their teaching, I have tried to describe how children's behaviours change on each task in the lesson from early (I), to middle (II), to late (III) stages. Grouping these changes into early, middle and late phases of a lesson series probably distorts the real picture for each individual because it does not reflect the range of individual differences or the continuous nature of the changes.

Further reading:
Clay (2001). *Change Over Time in Children's Literacy Development.*
Dyson, A.H. (1990), Weaving possibilities: Rethinking metaphors for early literacy development. *The Reading Teacher*, 44, 3, pp. 202–13.
Clay (1991a). *Becoming Literate: The construction of inner control,*
chapter 11.
Clay (1993a). *Reading Recovery: A guidebook for teachers in training*, p. 17.

---

1   Rereading familiar books

This task provides for volume of reading practice, speeded recognition, acquaintance with a wide range of texts, structures and meanings, orchestration of processing, and the understanding of stories.

I   The child gives attention to concepts about print, direction, and the linking of print and speech. Becomes aware of, and uses, the visual features of language in print while still managing to read a story. This rereading will challenge aspects of his processing. A good reading at this level will sound good.

II   The processing shifts to more effective fluent reading of increasingly difficult texts. Several strategic activities are used on known words and phrases. If any information source appears to dominate (meaning, or structure or print-sound relationships) this may signal that one type of information is being used separately rather than in combination with other types.

III   Longer and more advanced texts are read faster with increasing independence and in a phrased and fluent way. The reader slows up to analyse what is new or not yet under control. Sub-systems support each other and meet challenges in alternative ways. Word and part-word processing is embedded in text reading on the run.

2   Rereading yesterday's new book

A behaviour record is taken of yesterday's new book, that is now being read for the second time with no teacher input.

I, II   The changes on familiar books (above) begin to appear on new books. The reader shows independent use of what was attended to yesterday. He uses a range of strategic activities — monitoring, choosing between alternatives, confirming or revising, and making appropriate links.

III   The behaviour record captures evidence of strategic activities including how well the child finds clusters of letters embedded within words while remaining attentive to the meaning of the text, to the structure of the language, and to pace. Strategic activities are smoothly integrated and the child is clearly reading continuous text.

3   Letter identification and breaking words into parts

I   Learns to identify letters by some means. Breaks apart known words (from reading or writing) into letters and identifies some of these. The child is learning that letter order and letter orientation are important.

II   Breaks words into single letters, or into clusters, or into onsets and rimes, and into larger chunks. Fast recognition of letter forms with fast links to sounds are observed.

- Moves left to right in sequence across the letters in words.
- Looks at the root, breaks off (or adds) final inflections.
- Learns to take off first letters, or clusters of consonants (onsets), and finds them in other words.
- Later, can take the rime away from the onset.

The child notices that the same letters or clusters are found in different words, and so can begin to use analogy.

III   The child understands more about the features of words and letters embedded in texts. He breaks up words in text in flexible ways on the run and on his own. *(The teacher should note down the details and reinforce the most useful of his attempts, rather than the most unusual or intriguing.)*

4   Writing a story or message

The child composes a message to be written, and teacher and child share the production.

I   The child learns to compose a message to be written. The child works on directional and spatial rules, learns to form letters, learns to hear the phonemes in words, monitors all aspects of the task, and begins to build a writing vocabulary.

II   Writing vocabulary (words known in every detail) expands steadily. The child understands how to use phonological analysis of his speech with some independence and also gives attention to some orthographic features.

III   The messages composed are more complex and varied. Phonological and orthographic analyses of words by the child on his own are more frequent, but he may not work aloud. Expect to see the child rehearse and trial words (or find a word to copy), and break new words into suitable chunks.

5   Hearing and recording sounds in words

Sound-to-letter links become consistent and rapid.

I   Gets some phonemes, at first in any position, but shifts to hearing the initial phoneme, and searches for the first letter. Begins to search from the beginning to end of the spoken word.

II   Able to hear most consonants (except 'buried ones' like 'l' in 'sold' and 'n' in 'went') and knows most letters. Now the child usually works left to right on letters and first-to-last on phonemes. Is gaining independence on regular spellings.

III   Able to hear most phonemes in words without help. Uses phonological analysis and demonstrates increasing awareness of regular orthographic features. Teacher input for new features of English is needed. Children will find the consistencies in language. Teachers must support the discovery of the inconsistencies in the written code.

6   Reconstructing the cut-up story

The child reconstructs the teacher's copy of the child's story.

I   The child can monitor but only on a few features of print. He attends to the order of words, sequences of letters, and links to his own language.

II Maintains control over the sentence, checks at the word level, particularly beginnings and endings, and corrects errors. Is able to pull words into phrases and may even put a phrase in a new position.

III Continues to explore the phonology and orthography of words, and shows faster perception, problem-solving, and flexibility in sentence and story construction, and phrasing.

7 Sharing the introduction to the new book

The text is not read. Teacher and child discuss plot and vocabulary, and rehearse language structures. (See Part Two, pp. 162–63, for a variation.)

I The child learns how to attend to and use the teacher's introduction to orient himself to the new book.

II As above but the child's contribution is greater. The interaction tells the teacher more about what the child is bringing to this story.

III The child has learned a great deal about how to orient himself to many aspects of the new text.

8 Attempting the new book

This is the first reading of a new book that was carefully selected to challenge this child.

I The learner applies what is known to new text, such as one-to-one matching and locating known words. The teacher helps.

II The child monitors, searches, discovers, cross-checks, repeats to confirm, and self-corrects. The novel text helps to reveal what is challenging the learner's processing system.

III Children solve new challenges including multisyllabic words within more difficult texts at speed, working with clusters of letters. Smoothly operating reading systems produce evidence of how the system is becoming self-extending.

The changes described link to Tables 1 and 3A in Clay (2001) *Change Over Time in Children's Literacy Development*, pp. 84–85 and 226–27. Reference is made above to early, middle and late behaviours. Early (I) refers to sections 1–2 of Table 1, middle (II) refers to sections 3–4, late (III) refers to 4–5. Behaviours described in section 6 of Table 1 are beyond the highest levels at which most students leave Reading Recovery.

6 Individual lessons are discontinued: the school team monitors for continuing progress

An early intervention for the lowest-achieving six-year-olds cannot aim to bring its children to the ultimate status of the good silent reader whose reading improves because he reads and whose writing improves because he writes. Those are the accomplishments of successful children in their third or fourth year of school.

Children who successfully complete early literacy interventions like Reading Recovery should operate in reading and writing in ways that put them on track for being silent readers with self-extending processing systems during the next two years at school. With good classroom instruction and moderate personal motivation that should be achievable.

The procedures in this guidebook were designed to develop the beginnings of a self-extending system from the first lessons (see Part Two).

The child's peers in his classroom have learned to read and write, through the effective processing they can already do. The classroom children have learned

- to detect errors for themselves,
- to search for more information,
- to monitor for errors,
- to correct those errors,
- to check a decision,
- if necessary to repeat,
- and to confirm a decision.

Contrast that with a child coming into Reading Recovery who has already put together a confused processing system. After 12 to 20 weeks of successful Reading Recovery such a child will have learned how to work effectively at problem-solving texts at some level, and the best will perform as well as their successful peers.

The decision to end individual support

As the time approaches for a particular child's Reading Recovery lessons to be discontinued his teacher will still be lifting the text difficulty levels in reading and encouraging more complexity in his writing. She will monitor progress closely and check for signs of the behaviours listed in chapter 5 on the higher level texts he is reading.

The child must have enough practice on texts at each higher level to consolidate new learning, and yet the teacher will be lifting the difficulty level of the texts she is selecting for him to read. Towards the end of the lesson series she will be under pressure to have the child reading the same texts as those used by his average classroom peers with a high degree of independence. During this time there is a risk that the child may not be given sufficient time to consolidate new learning.

The child should be working at or above Level 16 of an approved list of text levels that has been field-tested. Some countries set the exit level as levels 18–20. And in some schools the child must be able to read well above Level 20 to fully participate in classroom activities with his average peers. Slightly lower exit levels are sometimes used for children who have made rapid progress to average levels for their age and/or class. However, Reading Recovery children who exit at low levels face *a high risk of not maintaining average progress*. If a child's programme is discontinued at or below Level 12 one cannot be confident about his subsequent progress.

About four weeks before a lesson series is to be discontinued it is essential that the Reading Recovery teacher and the class teacher discuss how the child performs in classroom routines and activities, and what needs to be done in the next few weeks to make the transition smooth.

The Reading Recovery teacher will prepare the child to succeed in that particular classroom in the final weeks of the lesson series.

Early strategic activities are effective

Reading Recovery teachers aim to produce independent readers whose reading and writing improve whenever they read and write. If the student is nearing the end of his lesson series he should be able to

- monitor his own reading and writing,
- anticipate a possible syntactic structure,
- search for differnt kinds of information in word sequences, in meaning and in sound-letter sequences,
- discover new things for himself,
- cross-check one source of information with another,
- repeat as if to confirm his reading or writing so far,
- use several sources of information together on the first attempt,
- self-correct taking the initiative for making decisions or getting words right in every respect,
- solve new words by these means.

Think about what the child cannot yet do

The child will need to have many different ways to approach print. Teachers should encourage flexibility in the sense that the child has several ways to solve text problems. Some of these ideas will prove helpful.

- Guide the child to predict what structures come next in the longer sentences in his text reading. Have him flexibly alter the arrangement of phrases in his cut-up story.
- Coach him how to hear difficult sound sequences in clusters of sounds, and buried within longer words.
- Demonstrate flexibility to him by breaking up words in several different ways.
- Encourage him to identify letters and clusters speedily.
- Show him how to approach multisyllabic words, shifting from sounding first letters to trying a syllabic attack first (perhaps returning to clapping syllables, briefly).
- Work hard to speed up sluggish motor responses that go with 'a slow decoding pace' (but do not put stress on the odd child who cannot work at speed). 'Slowness' may occur because of how the eyes scan the print, or unnecessary pointing, or speaking slowly in 'a reading voice', as a habit that goes with the reading situation.
- Attend to strengthening all aspects of writing, especially composing.

Think of ways to develop more effective processing systems for this particular reader and writer, and work on how he can be more effective at pulling different sources of information together.

A change in the support given to the child

The decision to discontinue must be weighed up very carefully.

The child has come a long way in a short time, but still has a long distance to travel to become a good reader and writer. *The transition to only classroom support must be made in such a manner that progress continues.*

The Reading Recovery teacher considers the issues and recommends to her colleagues in the school team that this child should be able to make progress from now on. Most children will manage the transition without close monitoring; but there will be one or two who need a temporary increase in attention from the classroom teacher to facilitate the change. Some personal help might be necessary if circumstances create a new demand that this child cannot deal with on his own.

Part of the success of Reading Recovery lessons is the close supervision the teacher has of the day-by-day changes in children's behaviour. Such individual help is not typical or even possible in a classroom because the teacher is managing several groups of children who are all moving on different time schedules. When Reading Recovery lessons end the class teacher will be taking all her children into new territory and week by week she will challenge their literacy processing skills further. The Reading Recovery teacher will need to prepare the child (whose special lessons will be discontinued) in several ways for working effectively without her tutoring help.

- **Sources of self-help**   Back in that classroom it would be ideal if the child could work on his own, confident enough to know when to appeal for help and how to use that help. Often he needs to be able to continue to increase his control over reading and writing with a 'not-noticing' teacher. The Reading Recovery teacher will *need to draw his attention to various sources of self-help back in the classroom.*

- **Being independent**   The Reading Recovery teacher has been preparing the child for this transfer throughout his whole lesson series. From his first lessons she has encouraged and reinforced independent operating, and problem detection, and problem-solving. Her teaching must avoid one common outcome of old-style remedial instruction: it is all too easy in individual tutoring for pupils to become dependent on the teacher. A Reading Recovery teacher must make children reasonably independent if they are to succeed in the everyday practice of reading and writing in their classrooms.

When the teacher recommends that supplementary help be discontinued she is making a prediction on the basis of her experience that this child will continue to make satisfactory progress. We would like to think that our predictions are reliable and rarely wrong but of course predicting is always open to some error. At this point if the teacher is not careful about this decision then she may deprive the child of extended help that he needs. *It is essential that decisions to discontinue the individual help are made to meet the child's learning needs, and not for the school's convenience, or because of district edicts, or to make the annual returns look better. This child's subsequent progress through education is at stake.*

Two positive outcomes

Now let us look at why Reading Recovery people claim that this programme has *two positive outcomes*. One positive outcome is for the child to be successful and for individual lessons to be discontinued. *The second positive outcome is to be referred for further assessment, for long-term assistance, and for specialist help.* Why is that positive?

Instead of struggling up through the next classes of the elementary school, never having caught up, the child who has made progress but has not reached the average levels of his class in his school is identified for further help. That help should be tailored to his current educational needs. Four or five months of individual instruction has provided evidence (in the form of diagnostic teaching) to add to any psychological test evidence that is available. Liaison between the Reading Recovery Tutors or Teacher Leaders and the referring agency, with sharing of records and test results, will usually be helpful. The careful assessment of reading and writing progress by Reading Recovery teachers helps specialists to identify appropriate further help for the learner. Immediate transfer from Reading Recovery to the next wave of help ensures that what has been learned so far will not be forgotten. The transfer to further help should be made immediately.

The more effective the education system is at delivering an early literacy intervention, the fewer children will need to be referred for further intensive help. Each education system records annually data on every child at entry to and exit from Reading Recovery. These reports show that the greatest economy in delivering an individual literacy intervention to young children is achieved when it can produce high discontinuing rates — 80 percent of the lowest achievers in strong implementations, rising to 90–95 percent in some cases — and low rates of referrals for continuing help.

It is clear from hundreds of implementation projects in very different education systems that when the economy of effectiveness is not achieved it is because there have been insufficient resources to serve the local needs. Well-trained teachers will produce the best results when funding allows for this.

Deciding when to discontinue lessons

How can we decide whether a child is ready for the individual tutoring to stop? There can be no hard and fast criteria because the aim will be to have a child work with a class group in which he can continue to make progress, and this will differ from child to child and from school to school.

Consultation with the class teachers, and the person in charge of the first years in school, will be necessary. Recording observations of the child's behaviour during class reading at any time during his Reading Recovery lesson series can be helpful but they are particularly important when decisions are being made about continuing or discontinuing tuition.

Reading Recovery teachers find it useful to consider the following issues when they are deciding whether individual lessons should be discontinued. (See Recommendations for Discontinuing Before Final Assessment, Part Two, Appendix, p. 195.) They write down what they are thinking about the child's progress so that they can discuss it with a colleague and check it with the results of an independently administered Observation Survey assessment.

Setting

Is there an appropriate group at his level towards the middle of his present class? Think about the size of the group, the book level at which they are working, their rate of progress, and the teacher's routines or practices. The child may enter a group at a level below the one he was working on with his Reading Recovery teacher.

Survival

How well will this child survive back in his class? Will he continue to learn from his own efforts? Can he participate in the classroom activities as his teacher would expect him to? Reading Recovery teachers must prepare a child for some of these things in the last weeks of his lesson series. What evidence do you have from the reading he does for you and the writing he does for you? Are reading and writing equally strong? To predict subsequent success you need to consider both.

Running Record analysis

Does the child read increasingly difficult material always at 90 percent accuracy or above? Does he read (easy) books for pleasure? Does he get opportunities to do this? Can he learn from his own efforts to problem-solve as he reads?

Writing process analysis

How independent is the child in composing, using resources to get to new words, monitoring and editing what he has done? Does he know when he needs help? Will he get that help?

Estimate of scores

Do you expect his scores to have improved on the tasks of the Observation Survey? (All the thinking discussed above has preceded retesting.) What evidence do you have to support this? Where was he weak before? Will he be able to score much higher now?

Observable behaviours to look for when withdrawing individual lessons

There is no fixed set of strategies, and no required levels of text, nor any test score that can guarantee successful progress after discontinuing. The higher the child's levels of competence in reading and writing, the better the predictions become, and the lower they are, the more risk you take with his future progress if you discontinue his lessons.

(The list that follows is discussed extensively in Part Two, p. 99 ff., in relation to progress midway through a lesson series. Here the same analysis is applied to higher levels of text.)

If the child is ready for the lesson series to end he will be able to control these things:

- *Directional movement*   The child will have control over this without lapses, or he will be aware of his tendency to lapse and will be able to check on his own behaviour.

- *One-to-one matching*   The child can adopt a controlled one-to-one matching of spoken to written words (and sequence of sounds in words) for checking purposes.

- *Strategic activities*   He can demonstrate a flexible control of strategic activity on new instructional texts at higher levels of difficulty. He will try to solve new words and new language structures in new texts.

- *Self-monitoring*   The child checks on himself (often unprompted). This can be seen when an error is noticed whether or not it is corrected. It is also observed as the child assembles a cut-up story.

- *Cross-checking*   The child notices discrepancies in his own responses by cross-checking one kind of information (say, visual) with a different kind of information (such as meaning). This is seen less often during later lessons.

- *Use of multiple sources of information*   Check self-corrections. It is sometimes clear that the child finds it easy to combine meaning, and structure, and letter-sound cues, and a sense of how words are spelled, and tries to achieve a match across all kinds of information.

- *Self-correction*   Effective self-correction follows from using self-monitoring, searching for solutions in flexible ways, and cross-checking information. However, even unsuccessful attempts at self-correction are indicators that the child is aware these activities can be helpful. In good readers self-correction may occur without much evidence that you can observe and record!

Questions of level

Usually the child who is ready for the lessons to end can read a text that the average child in his second year at school can read (see pp. 52–53 in this chapter). He can write two or three complex sentences for his story, requiring help from his teacher with only one or two words. Check the record of words he writes independently and the stories he writes. Make sure there has been marked improvement and that strategies of getting from letters to sounds and sounds to letters have developed.

If discontinuing lessons ...

As the next step in discontinuing prepare the child and his class teacher for this, perhaps even working with the child in his classroom for the last two weeks of his series of lessons.

Then have the child tested on the Observation Survey by an independent tester (for example, another teacher who has been trained to do this) and analyse the strengths and weaknesses at this point in time. Compare them with any earlier testing and note the areas in which progress occurred. At this point decide finally to discontinue.

Discuss the child's current status with his class teacher, again

It is often advisable to offer to monitor the child's progress, say once every two weeks, then once a month, until you and his teacher are sure that he is continuing to make progress. You may take a Running Record every two weeks on the books the child is reading in his class, and also discuss his progress in writing with the teacher. Talk over a particular piece of work. A steady increase in the length and complexity of the writing is needed.

The child may need a few scheduled, individual text reading sessions with 'a competent other' to sustain his confidence and motivation during the transition period. This may be to increase his fluency, or as a check on progress, *and to build up the sheer quantity of careful reading that he needs to do* in order to continue to progress. When Reading Recovery lessons are discontinued some children may react with new doubts about their ability to cope.

Perhaps the school monitors progress in some regular way that allows the Reading Recovery teacher to check the progress of her students.

If not discontinuing lessons ...

The teacher and the Reading Recovery team at the school may make a decision that:

- The child needs to continue Reading Recovery for a limited period (state the number of weeks).
- The child needs further help in two or three areas where he is still weak, such as text reading, or hearing sounds in sequence, or taking words apart, or writing new words, or solving new words in reading.

- The teacher must set new learning goals to make the child independent. Continue only as long as necessary. Make new plans for discontinuing, testing only in the critical areas on this second occasion.

- The decision may be that the child will need further specialist help before he can progress with the class instruction only. *If so make the referral and work hard to arrange his transfer to a new support system.* Explain this to everyone as a positive outcome because the period of teaching has uncovered this need. It has provided diagnostic information on how this child learns. Stress the urgency of providing further assistance.

Follow-up and check-up

Research studies that have followed children who had remedial instruction have often reported that progress was not maintained back in the classroom. Research following up Reading Recovery children shows that, in general, progress is sustained for most of the children. However, in New Zealand studies some children who made slow progress for the first year after Reading Recovery, accelerated again in the following year, and other children began to lag in progress after two years.

The numbers of such children are small but they lead us to recommend that Reading Recovery teachers or some other teacher should be given the role:

- to monitor progress sensitively over the next three years,
- and to provide further individual help if needed if progress slows down.

Although Reading Recovery children perform well in their classes some of them remain at-risk children, easily thrown by life circumstances or by subsequent learning experiences of poor quality. A refresher course of individual instruction for quite a short period should be most helpful for a child who has begun to slip behind his classmates.

> *Further reading:*
> Clay, *Reading Recovery: A guidebook for teachers in training* (1993a) contains reports of the early research on Reading Recovery in New Zealand.

Using literacy to build literacy

How do we know when we can leave it to the learner, the school and the environment to foster further literacy learning? When can we discontinue the Reading Recovery support? It is not economically possible to continue to provide individual lessons until we can be sure of the child's future success. That is why we have these dilemmas about continuing or not continuing the individual lesson support system.

We have heard that 'you learn to read by reading'. We can think about the implications of a statement that says 'This child read 30 books in the last three months but this other child read 300.' It is easy for a Reading Recovery teacher who understands the reciprocity of reading and writing for strengthening the child's strategic activity with the written language, to understand a similar statement that says 'you learn to write by writing'.

Once our brains have learned to deal with a degree of complexity in written language, use of that language expands our repertoire and the things we can do with written language. In the environments of schools and communities that value reading and writing, young children get better and better at strengthening and stretching or expanding the neural systems that make them able to attend to written language.

The child has two transitions to make as supplementary help is withdrawn. The first is a transition from individual support lessons to managing to continue to progress in the classroom. The second is to become a silent reader whose strategic activity is flexible and tentative enough to learn to work with more and more of the complexities of language from all kinds of reading and writing experiences.

One key to making a success of both these transitions could be discussed under the heading of 'independence'. A Reading Recovery position on independent activity would be an activity that the child initiates and carries out on his own. This is encouraged from the very beginning of lessons in that the teacher never does anything for the child that he could do for himself. Where teachers share and help to complete a task, the child is expected to carry out whatever he can do independently and he knows this is expected of him.

Independence is not taught. It is an outcome of an activity when a child controls that bit of processing and the teacher knows she can hold off that emphasis and move to another. Children do not take on reading and writing processes without help. Someone from the culture must provide opportunities for them to become active and interested. The teacher provides high levels of demonstration and support when necessary, and less support when appropriate. She makes choices about what the learner attends to next and chooses books and words and tasks to be worked on in writing and reading. (This is a very important part of instruction but is not always seen as such.) She also has the knowledge and expectation of how well the child has taken over the ownership of using his reading and writing to extend his skills in both those activities.

The teacher cannot 'teach' independence. She sets up fail-safe situations within which the child can initiate successful activity! The child will succeed and the teacher invites the child to do so. Teachers do not need to know how to teach independence: they need to know how and when to hold back and let the independent child take over the whole task. Children learn that this is expected very quickly. It is often the teacher who finds it difficult to let the child be independent; she finds it difficult to be asked not to teach.

So the child who has completed a series of Reading Recovery lessons is going to have to continue to learn with much less support. He has to be able to act independently in his classroom. Sometimes he will have to solve his own problems, sometimes he will have to interact with another child to get or give help, sometimes he will have to participate with others in a group and sometimes he will have to know how and when to get help from the teacher. And it will be important that he has some measure of independence in both writing and reading. For it will be one of his resources to know that what he knows in reading may help him with his writing and vice versa.

The book level at which this child can read when Reading Recovery lessons are discontinued is no more than a signpost that perhaps he will be able to continue to extend his literacy powers. The signpost is not reliable. It may be pointing in the right direction but it does not indicate the length of time or the conditions under which he will travel and arrive safely.

Similarly, a score of around 40 very different words for writing vocabulary may encourage you to believe that this child has an adequate foundation for future writing progress but do not be too sure. I know of teachers who have coached children to get high writing scores by teaching or prompting three-letter words. What children need is to know how to get to new words (in their own speech) using bits and pieces of that core writing vocabulary they use when writing their stories. A varied writing vocabulary gives the child a better base from which to build further English words.

The essence of success with discontinuing judgements is whether the teacher can be confident that this child does discover things for himself, works out some possibilities, and extends his own processing skills in both reading and writing. And that he enjoys the challenge of doing this.

As the child reaches out to more complex texts and writes longer and more involved stories these operations will be used with increasing speed and fluency on:

- longer stretches of meaning
- less familiar language
- less predictable texts.

And in the end
it is the individual adaptation
made by the expert teacher
to that child's idiosyncratic competencies
and history of past experiences
that starts him on the upward climb
to effective literacy performances.

References

Ashdown, J. and Simic, O. (2000). Is early literacy intervention effective for English language learners?: Evidence from Reading Recovery. In S. Forbes and C. Briggs (eds), *Research in Reading Recovery*, Vol. 2, pp. 115–32. Portsmouth, New Hampshire: Heinemann.

Bissex, G. (1980). *GNYS AT WRK: A child learns to write and read.* Cambridge, Massachusetts: Harvard University Press.

Breznitz, Z. and Share, D. (2002). Introduction to a theme of 'Timing and Phonology'. *Reading and Writing: An international journal*, 15: 1–2 (February).

Cazden, C. (2004). Teaching Literacy. *Bank Street Alumni News Digest*, Fall: 18, 25–27.

Clay, M.M. (1972). *Reading: The patterning of complex behaviour*, second edition 1979. Auckland: Heinemann.

—— (1974). The spatial characteristics of the open book. *Visible Language*, 8, 3: 275–82.

—— (1979 US reprint, 1975). *What Did I Write?* Auckland: Heinemann; Portsmouth, New Hampshire: Heinemann.

—— (1982). *Observing Young Readers: Selected papers.* Portsmouth, New Hampshire: Heinemann.

—— (1985). *The Early Detection of Reading Difficulties,* third edition. Auckland: Heinemann.

—— (1987). *Writing Begins at Home.* Auckland: Heinemann.

—— (1987). Implementing Reading Recovery: Systemic adaptations to an educational innovation. *New Zealand Journal of Educational Studies*, 22, 1: 35–58.

—— (1990). The Reading Recovery Programme, 1984–88: Coverage, outcomes and Education Board figures. *New Zealand Journal of Educational Studies*, 25, 1: 61–70.

—— (1991a). *Becoming Literate: The construction of inner control.* Auckland: Heinemann.

—— (1991b). Introducing a storybook to young readers. *The Reading Teacher*, 45, 4: 264–73.

—— (1993a). *Reading Recovery: A guidebook for teachers in training.* Auckland: Heinemann.

—— (2005, 2002, 1993b). *An Observation Survey of Early Literacy Achievement.* Auckland: Heinemann.

—— (1998). *By Different Paths to Common Outcomes.* York, Maine: Stenhouse.

———— (2001). *Change Over Time in Children's Literacy Development.* Auckland: Heinemann.

Clay, M.M., Gill, M., Glynn, T., McNaughton, T. and Salmon, K. (1983). *Record of Oral Language and Biks and Gutches.* Auckland: Heinemann.

Clay, M.M. and Tuck, B. (1993). A Study of Reading Recovery Subgroups: Including outcomes for children who did not satisfy discontinuing criteria. In Clay, M.M., *Reading Recovery: A guidebook for teachers in training,* first edition, pp. 86–95.

Clay, M.M. and Watson, B. (1982). The Success of Maori Children in the Reading Recovery Programme. Report to the Director of Research, Department of Education, Wellington.

Dyson, A.H. (1984). Research Currents: Who controls classroom writing? *Language Arts,* 61, 6: 442–62.

———— (1990). Weaving possibilities: Rethinking metaphors for early literacy development. *The Reading Teacher*, 44, 3: 202–13.

Ehri, L.C. and Sweet, J. (1991). Fingerpoint-reading of memorised text: What enables beginners to process the print? *Reading Research Quarterly* 26, 4: 442–62.

Fernald, G.M. (1943). *Remedial Techniques in Basic School Subjects.* New York: McGraw-Hill.

Ferreiro, E. (2003). *Past and Present of the Verbs to Read and Write: Essays on literacy.* Toronto: Douglas and McIntyre.

Gentile, L.M. (1997). Oral language assessment and development in Reading Recovery in the United States. In S.L. Swartz and A.F. Klein (eds), *Research in Reading Recovery,* Vol. 1: 187–96. Portsmouth, New Hampshire: Heinemann.

Glynn, T., Crookes, T., Bethune, N., Ballard, K. and Smith, J. (1989). *Reading Recovery in Context.* Report to Research Division, Ministry of Education, Wellington.

Goodman, K.S. and Burke, C.L. (1973, April). Theoretically based studies of patterns of miscues in oral reading performance (Project No. 9–0375). Washington, DC: US Office of Education.

Greenfield, S. (2000). *Brain Story.* London: BBC Worldwide.

Hatcher, P. (1994). An integrated approach to encouraging the development of phonological awareness, reading and writing. In C. Hulme and M. Snowling (eds), *Reading Development and Dyslexia.* San Diego, California: Singular Publishing, pp. 163–80.

Hobsbaum, A. (1997). Reading Recovery in England. In S.L. Swartz and A.F. Klein (eds), *Research in Reading Recovery,* Vol. l: 132–47. Portsmouth, New Hampshire: Heinemann.

Hobsbaum, A., Peters, S. and Sylva, K. (1996). Scaffolding in Reading Recovery. *Oxford Review of Education*, 22, 1: 17–35.

Iversen, S.J. (1991). Phonological processing skills and the Reading Recovery programme. MA dissertation, Massey University Library, Palmerston North, New Zealand.

———— (1997). Reading Recovery as a small group intervention. Unpublished doctoral dissertation, Massey University, Palmerston North, New Zealand.

Johnston, P.H. (2004). *Choice Words: How language affects children's learning.* Portland, Maine: Stenhouse Publishing.

Jones, N., Johnson, C., Schwartz, R.M. and Zalud, G. (2005). Two positive outcomes of Reading Recovery: Exploring the interface between Reading Recovery and Special Education. *The Journal of Reading Recovery*, 4, 3: 19–34.

Joseph, L.M. (1999). Word boxes help children with learning disabilities identify and spell words. *The Reading Teacher*, 52, 4: 348–57.

Kamii, C. and Manning, M. (2002). Phonemic awareness and beginning reading and writing. *Journal of Research in Childhood Education*, 17, 1: 38–46.

Kaye, E.L. (2002). Variety, complexity and change in reading behaviours of second grade students. Doctoral dissertation, Texas Woman's University.

Kuhn, M.R. and Stahl, S. (2003). Fluency: A review of developmental and remedial practices. *Journal of Educational Psychology*, 95, 1: 3–21.

Litt, D.G. (2003). An exploration of the double-deficit hypothesis in the Reading Recovery population. Doctoral dissertation: University of Maryland.

Lyons, C.A. (1991). Helping a learning-disabled child enter the literate world. In D.E. Deford, C.A. Lyons and G.S. Pinnell (eds), *Bridges to Literacy: Learning from Reading Recovery.* Portsmouth, New Hampshire: Heinemann, pp. 205–16.

———— (1994). Reading Recovery and learning disability issues, challenges and implications. *Literacy, Teaching and Learning: An international journal of literacy learning*, 1: 109–20.

———— (2003). *Teaching Struggling Readers: How to use brain-based research to maximise learning.* Portsmouth, New Hampshire: Heinemann.

McLane, J.B. and McNamee, G.D. (1990). *Early Literacy.* Cambridge, Massachusetts: Harvard University Press.

Neal, J.C. and Kelly, P.R. (1999). The success of Reading Recovery for English language learners and Descubriendo La Lectura for Bilingual Students in California. In S. Forbes and C. Briggs (eds), *Research in Reading Recovery*, Vol. 2, pp. 115–32. Portsmouth, New Hampshire: Heinemann.

Nodelman, P. (2001). 'A' is for … what? The function of alphabet books. *Journal of Early Childhood Literacy*, 1, 3: 235–54.

O'Leary, S. (1997). *Five Kids.* Bothell, Washington: The Wright Group.

Pearson, P.D. (2000). Ohio Reading Recovery Conference address. See Clay, M. (2005), Stirring the water again. *The Journal of Reading Recovery*, 4, 3: 1–10.

Pinker, S. (2000). *Words and Rules: The ingredients of language.* London: Phoenix.

Pinnell, G.S., DeFord, D.E. and Lyons, C.A. (1988). *Reading Recovery: Early intervention for at-risk first graders.* Arlington, Virginia: Educational Research Service.

Randell, B. (2000). *Shaping the PM Story Books.* Wellington: Gondwanaland Press.

Rayner, K. and Juhasz, B. (2004). Eye movements in reading: Old questions and new directions. *European Journal of Cognitive Psychology*, 16, 1–2: 349.

Rodgers, E. (2000). Language matters: When is a scaffold really a scaffold? *National Reading Conference Yearbook*, 49: 78–90.

Schmitt, M.C., Askew, B.J., Fountas, I.C. and Pinnell, G.S. (2005). *Changing Futures: The influence of Reading Recovery in the United States.* Columbus, Ohio: The Reading Recovery Council of North America.

Schwartz, R.M. (1997). Self-monitoring in beginning reading. *The Reading Teacher*, 51, 1: 40–51.

——— (2005). Decisions, decisions: Responding to primary students during guided reading. *The Reading Teacher*, 58, 5: 436–43.

Smith, P. (2005). Self-monitoring and the acquisition of literacy. Doctoral dissertation submitted: University of Auckland, Auckland.

Swanson, H.L., Trainin, G., Mecoechaea, D.M. and Hammill, D.D. (2004). Rapid naming, phonological awareness, and reading: A meta-analysis of correlation evidence. *Review of Educational Research*, 73, 4: 407–40.

Tunmer, W.E. and Chapman, J.W. (2003). The Reading Recovery approach to preventive early intervention. As good as it gets? *Reading Psychology*, 24: 345 ff.

Weaver, C.A., Mannes, S. and Fletcher, C.R. (1995). *Discourse Comprehension: Essays in honor of Walter Kintsch.* Hillsdale, New Jersey: Lawrence Erlbaum.

Wong, S.D., Groth, L.A., and O'Flahavan, J.F. (1994). *Characterizing teacher-student interaction in Reading Recovery lessons.* Universities of Georgia and Maryland: National Reading Research Center Report, No. 17.

Index

Contents of Part Two